G000045265

CRIES FROM
CASEMENT
AS HIS BONES
ARE BROUGHT
TO DUBLIN

CRIES FROM CASEMENT AS HIS BONES ARE BROUGHT TO DUBLIN

British Broadcasting Corporation

Published by the
British Broadcasting Corporation
35 Marylebone High Street
London W1M 4AA

First published 1974

© David Rudkin 1974

ISBN 0 563 12644 2

All rights whatsoever in this play
are strictly reserved and
application for performance,
etc., should be made before
rehearsal to Margaret Ramsay Ltd,
14A Goodwins Court, St Martin's Lane,
London WC2. No performance may be given
unless a licence has been obtained.

Printed in England by
Tonbridge Printers Ltd,
Peach Hall Works, Tonbridge, Kent

Author's Note

This is a reading version of my *Casement* text
as used in the original production. There
are however a few emendations, and I should mention
these: some inaccuracies of history
put right, a few cuts restored, minor excisions
made. I do not pretend to have prepared a
playscript for the theatre – thoughts on
possible ways of staging I confine to an
appendix. I wish this text to stand as a
testament to a broadcast that realized
my purpose with a marvellous insight and
fidelity.

D R

Cries from Casement as his bones are brought to Dublin
was first broadcast in BBC Radio 3 on 4 February 1973.
The play was produced by John Tydeman and the part of
Roger Casement played by Norman Rodway. Other
parts were played by Joan Bakewell, Sean Barrett,
Kate Binchy, Michael Deacon, William Eedle,
Kevin Flood, Martin Friend, Heather Gibson,
David Gooderson, Sheila Grant, Michael Harbour,
John Hollis, Fraser Kerr, Rolf Lefebvre,
Peggy Marshall, Meryl O'Keefe, Irene Prador,
David Rudkin, Henry Stamper, Eva Stuart, John Tusa,
David Valla, Mary Wimbush and Joy Worth.

There is a full list of parts at the end
of the book.

I

An Actor with a *neutral voice*	Who's Who. Sir Roger Casement: QM, CMG, Knight. Born county Dublin eighteen-sixty-four, father a soldier, Ulster Protestant, mother a secret Catholic. School, Ballymena. University, none.
An Actor with an *English voice*	Distinguished career in Foreign and Intelligence services of Victorian and Edwardian Empire. E.g. eighteen-ninety-two, Assistant Surveyor to Niger Protectorate; eighteen-ninety-four, acting vice-consul, steps taken to stemp* out local human secrifice. Eighteen-ninety-nine, personal schemes to frustrate Imperial Germany's anti-British manoeuvrings in Boer War. Nineteen hundred, Queen's Medal for service in Saith Efrica.
Neutral	Nineteen-hundred-and-three, investigates and documents slave-labour atrocities in Belgian Congo rubber colonies.
English	Nineteen-eoh-five, Companion of the Order of Sint Michael and Sint George.
Neutral	Nineteen-hundred-and-ten, investigates atrocities in rubber colonies of Portuguese Amazon.
English	Knighted.
Neutral	Nineteen-fourteen, the Great War: Casement moves freely in Germany as Kaiser's guest, recruiting an anti-British Brigade among Irish POWs there; negotiating German military assistance for a rebellion in Ireland.
An Actress with *an Irish voice*	April the twenty-first nineteen-sixteen: lands on Ireland's south-west coast with fruit of his mission. Arrested within hours; brought to London; interrogated; imprisoned in Tower; tried; hanged.
English	Judicial process perfectly proper.
Irish	On paper.

(*Pause*)

Neutral	Diaries. 'Black Diaries' so-called. A sodomite journal, purporting to be Casement's: leaked to press before and during trial; circulated internationally after, countering world agitation for a reprieve.
English	For forty-three years thereafter, the Heome Office find it

---

* Apparent errors are to be pronounced as spelt.

7

would be against the public interest to yield to presshah and confirm whether or not the Diaries in fact exist.

Neutral Nineteen-fifty-nine, a pirate transcript is published in Paris.

English Nineteen-fifty-nine, the Heome Secretary of the Day agrees to make the Diaries available, for limited inspection, by persons approved.

Irish Casement's body. Committed to the Pentonville limepit—previous incumbent, Crippen. Requests for return of his remains to Ireland, over a period of forty-nine years repeatedly refused.

Neutral And then, one day—

Crier (*vulgar, like stage Cockney music-hall MC*) Oyez, oyez!

(*Growd hubbub, crier's bell*)

Give eah! Give eah to mee—

Announceress (*cool, somewhat honky*) October nineteen-sixty-faw.

Crier Thank you, thank you. Forasmuch as the great British Public—namely your good muttonheaded selves – have at last awoke from yer ma'erial and carnal stupor, and elected a government – namely me – theore'ically pledged to the cause o' class peace, the abolishment o' wages and the rule of wealth – above all, radical dynamic change – be it therefore heard by you, that we, H M G, intend, as a curry to the Irish immigrant working class – on whom our economy so much depends, also, to be fair, because we've held on to the bloody things so long, they're not even symbolic for us any more – intend, I say, that at an appropriate time there shall be dug up for dispatch to Dublin, for such treatment as that coven o' run-down bookies the Irish Parliament shall fink fit, a chest of sulphura'ed and potassified remains, to which we shall affix the label ROGER CASEMENT!

British Public Who?

Crier Thanks be to Gawd and H M G – but most of all to H M G – that we of England know the meaning of mercy – even if we dispense it partially and too late; and in our dealings wiv neighbours display great prudence and sagaci'ee – even if only long after circumstance has left us wiv no other choice. But at least let it now be hoped, that wiv this gesture – which to England means damn-all but to the Irish much – wiv this gesture, I say, please Gawd, Gawd, please! we shall at last have washed our 'ands of the problem of Ireland for ever?

Man in the Street If you want to do that, mate, put all the Irish in a box, shove it aht to sea and sink it!

(Briefest truncated soundclip of multitudinous laughter)
(Silence)

II

(Tentative tappings on prison pipes: gather, grow, complexify . . .)

Announceress Tuesday February the twenty-third nineteen-sixty-five. Morning. The limepit at Pentonville, where Casement and Crippen lie.

(Tappings reach climax. Cut off. After brief pause)

Crippen *(stage Cockney)* Hey. Hey, you. Oy, you, nine nine one two. HalfPaddy rise and shine. Wakey, wakey, hands off your cock and reach for a sock. *(obscene croon:)* Hey, fruity boy . . . Casement . . .! Roger, sir . . .

Casement *(heard waking – Sudden cries of dread)*

Crippen *(stills him)* Hey, hey . . .! Not come to hang ya. All over and done with, that is: fifty years ago . . . All the same, halfPaddy: news for ya . . .

Casement *(stage Ulster)* It'll have to be brave and good. You have interrupted me again. A sauncy young fella of a fusilier was openin his thighs for me.

Crippen Oy oy oy oy, oy, oy, oy; does that have to be your first remark?

Casement I must die up till my black reputation.

Crippen Quiet; you'll upset your admirers.

Casement Ours will be no dialogue for admirers. Man dear, but God or whoever must have his tongue in his cheek, to have me end up on my last endless bed with the likes of you.

9

Crippen No marriages in Paradise, mate. 'Eternally yours' . . .
Only, not so: we're to be pah'ed. You're going back.
They're sending you back.

Casement (*heart leaps*) To Brazil—?

Crippen Hey ey, enough of that. None o your nice young tropical
fun-pals where you're going. Ireland, friend. They're
coming this mornin. To dig you up.

Casement I thought Crippen was a quiet-spoken doctor of a man.

Crippen We fought Casement was a gentle parfit knight.

(*Spades delve*)

Lynch (*west of Ireland speech*) Officer Mahoney, how shall we be
sure we dig up all the one man?

Mahoney (*adenoidal Dublin*) How do yous mean?

Lynch Not minus something, or plus parts of another?

Mahoney You know the official line on that: impossible.

Lynch But Officer Mahoney, I see what I can see. And what I see
is, 'tis anybody's guess what's goin in this box.

Mahoney It's the thought that counts. Here. These bones'll do.

(*Brief formalized tearing of bones*)

Lynch Officer Mahoney, do you think he really done those
things?

Mahoney What things?

Lynch Things.

Mahoney Wi boys an that?

Lynch I'm after readin in a book, his diaries . . . Them Peruvian
boys, he said some o them has you-know-what on them
an entire foot length. An tree inches across. Tree
inches!

Mahoney Go to God.

Lynch A whole foot length!

Mahoney There's little left to any of them now, an that's the long
an short an t'ick o that. Here—

(*More tearing-up of bones. Cries of Casement, mortally riven.
Soon also, from Crippen screams of offended rage*)

Crippen Hey! Hey! You two, watch it, *watch it*! My bleedin foot
you got there, me leg . . . Him you want, not me – Hey,
watch it – *Watch it*! AHHH—!

(Climax of bone-rending: Crippen's, Casement's screams. Cut. A guitar-chord, peremptory)

Balladeer *(recitative)*
> Some will call it a just irony,
> Others a typically macabre Irish farce,
> For her hero to be brought to his homeland at last,
> A poisoner's toe up his skeletal arse.

(Guitar-dissonance, left unresolved)

III

(Soft summery sounds, a lark etc.)

Announceress A Warwickshire orchard. In a small caravan he uses as a studi-eo, the Author drafts a play on Casement, wrestling with the riddle of the man.

Author *(voice Oxford with sufficient Ulster tinge)* A contrast of messages. One: March nineteen-hundred. From Casement, Cape Town, to Foreign Office, London, a dispatch.

Casement *(jingo)* A certain renegade Irish Major, MacBride by name, is in the pay of the Boers, and moving freely among their Irish prisoners of war, in an endeavour to recruit from them, for service against Her Majesty, a so-called Irish Brigade. This shows the despicable lengths to which Her Majesty's enemies will go, to induce men loyal to their Queen to be false to their allegiance and dishonour their oaths.

Author Message Two: March nineteen-sixteen. From German Foreign Office, Berlin, Wilhelmstrasse seventy-six, to German Embassy, New York, U S A, a dispatch.

German voice Casement's recruitment of Irish Brigade at Limburg prison camp proceeds. He proposes also their use help drive the British out of Egypt.

Author A turnabout. Inside that consular Victorian imperialistic shell, what hidden rebel seed? And what touch quickens it? What brooding makes an egg of it? What hatches it?

(Footfalls slowly echo down vaulted corridor of stone)

Announceress Public Records Office, London.

> (*A heavy inner door is opened. A strongroom door is unlocked, opened*)

Chalmers (*Cambridge voice*) You just wish to see the diaries?
Author I am researching for a play.
Chalmers Yes, we know that. There are five diaries.
Author (*simply*) Yes.

> (*A cabinet is unlocked, opened*)

(*sotto*) Casement. Forgive me: that I approach these, the properties of your possession, the secrets of your heart and flesh. (*aloud*) I'd like to see them all first, if I may; then take them in order, one by one. (*sotto*) Casement? You are with me. Your dead hand cannot reach me. Yet I fear it.
Chalmers Here we are. Nineteen-o-one – Field Service Notepad—
Author Red; slim; closing lengthways; with ribbon and strap. Typed endorsement: 'Army Book one-five-three, formerly property of Roger Casement, forwarded to Home Office by Police Commissioner – See correspondence, file three-one-one-six-four-three stroke two-o-six A.'
Chalmers Nineteen-o-three . . . Letts' Pocket Diary . . .
Author Black, roughly octavo, one inch thick. Same endorsement, 'property of Casement, file three-one-one etc. . . .'
Chalmers Nineteen-ten diary, nineteen-eleven ledger, nineteen-eleven diary proper . . .
Author Casement? Casement? I touch. I open. You are nowhere near. I feel nothing.
Congo. First Atrocity Investigation. O-one diary fragmentary: preliminary journey. O-three diary fuller: investigation itself. Notes for a scene. Congolese music authentic; Casement jingo-voiced.
Casement (*jingo*) Bad day today. Row with carriers. Seedy all day. Sandflies hateful. Beastly heat.

> (*High electronic heat-hum or subtle vibrance gradually supervenes*)

When I get back to Leo, must remember to ask if Mrs Bentley's watches got sent on. If not, arrange.
Rum thing in Brussels paper the other day. Article

claiming Westminster MPs ganged up on new member – background not up to scratch, it seemed. Physically kicked him out, four days running: only admitted him finally because of sporting spirit in which he took it all. How could we really be masters of the world if our government behaved as childishly as that? What was the headline? 'England the Land of Sport and Cant.' Funny notions about us some nations have.

Secretly, of course, they envy us. Our integrity. Our honour.

(Tropical thunder, downpour)

No sleep last night. Huge centipede all over curtain, enormous. Then it disappeared; I lay in dread . . .

(Downpour-thrash, hiss)

Rain in quantities, lifting in clouds. Timany boy from Kimbanga looking for work. In chains. A certain James Kudjoe off the steamer; for work; in chains . . .

(Downpour-drips. Drying)

. . . Kisantu. Madimba. Why so empty? Five women to one man. The men, where are they?
. . . Sukolela. Body of beheaded boy. Nothing done. Headache all day. Boloba: *(hint of Ulster voice)* a regular town, lots offer it there – Sh.

(Soft fresh liquid junglebird calls)

Bongandi. Left camp six fifty-eight-and-a-half a.m. Beautiful morning for the old Queen's birthday . . . Dreadful stories here of ill-treatment by Lake Leopold. There's a fine fellow, look, Egyptian ibis, black body, white wings: lovely fellow . . . Up from his Home in the woods below . . . Home . . .

(Heat-hum, vibrance)

Lukolela. Ikoko. A native desert. Nkaki. Ikakima. Whole families staggering from work in chains. Horrid business. Ikanga: five people with their hands cut off. Infamous. Infamous. I'll see we British get this stink stamped out.

13

(Drums)

And here he is: the stink himself. Monsieur Lejeim, taskmaster. The gall of him, to put on tonight a cultural display of native dance because tomorrow is my birthday!

(Congolese dance-music, authentic, pp throughout)

Thirty-nine . . . Middle age . . . Oh Juan, only twenty . . . Pepe, seventeen, his young down . . . Manuel, Accraman – (*faint hint of Ulster tinge*) Boys, Accraman's was enormous. Only on a spit the like of that would I be at home – (*English*) Quiet, Casement. There's a knighthood in this. Ay. In this million square miles of jungle the tortured black can expect no passer-by to hear his screams nor smell his burning flesh, but me. A knight to his rescue. 'Arise, Sir Roger.' Casement, KT. The royal sword.

No. No. Not glory. Not glory I seek. Nor honour like that. The Queen's Medal I've never worn. As much in my own right am I here. What right is that? As Casement myself. What self is that? What brief is that?

To help lift terror from a people's eyes, a people changed, a people on whom a nightmare has come, a havoc to hunt them in their own lands and savage them, atrocify.

Don't think M. Lejeim, butcher of blacks and lover of their art, don't think I cannot see. The evidence is on these naked bodies in the firelight as they dance, even a Prince couldn't miss it: the men, the women, the children; the young black men. Scars, weals, burns. I've eyes in my head.

What eyes, but? Consular eyes? British eyes . . .?

(Cut music)
(Vague murmur as of many natives waiting outside)

September first. Thirty-nine today. My fortieth year. I have fought a good fight, I have finished my course . . . Here's a fine lad they bring to me. Or *was* fine. Flogmarks. *Hippo* hide? Buttocks slashed; bowels exposed. He thinks I am a man with magic ointment, he begs soothing for his sores. He turns his crutch to me. Black scrotum, slit.

What eye is this that opens in my head? It sees two men. In this ripped manlihood it spies two men. King Leopold of Belgium, pink throned pig. In your own person vested all this Congo State. You fatten on its gold. Its gold is rubber. Its rubber is this black flesh. I see Your Belgic Majesty gorge in a gulp the total harvest of this one fellow's only, butchered life, to spend him in one royal fart.

(*faint hint of Ulster speech developing*) I see another man. No conqueror, no burner nor torturer with axe nor flail; no masterer. But a man, a me, spawned on the underbench of nature, part of him hunted himself; a Casement, would touch these ebony curves of Adam-flesh, ay, wants them whole, to touch, feel; kiss . . . That makes ye jump, King! Which King jump? Leopold I harry, Edward I serve? Jump, both. Casement wants these Congolese slit knackers knit and whole; for milk, for me . . . Leopold, Edward, White Christendom, rape Africa, plunder her of her nature's treasure, rubber, diamonds, ivory and gold. Oh Africa rape me, I'll ransack your gorgeous nature's-treasure dry, of milk, in me. – Hush hush, rob's colony, cock's felony. English again.

(*Cut murmurings*)

IV

(*Rain. Hum, whine of airfield*)

Announceress February the twenty-third nineteen-sixty-five. The coffin bearing the remains of some of Casement, and Crippen's leg, is brought from Pentonville in a car, to Northeolt Airfield; here, placed aboard an aircraft, Sint Flannan, of the Irish Fleet.

(*Inside aircraft: hum, whine, vibration of waiting to take off. Intercom switches on, crackle of static*)

Irish air hostess (*ladling a grotesque Irish charm*) Ladies and gentlemen, good afternoon. The Captain and crew of the Saint Flannan welcome Sir Roger Casement aboard their aircraft for the flight to Dublin. It is estimated that the flight-time will be one-and-a-half hours, during which we shall be cruising at a height of eleven thousand feet. We have pleasure meanwhile in providing for his entertainment a programme of Gaelic songs, interspersed with meditations on the spirit and the flesh, by Father MacEnroe of the Community of the Milk of Our Lady of Knock.

(*Harp and Woman*)

Crippen   Hey. Hey. You. HalfPat.

Casement   (*stage Ulster voice throughout*) Ay. Whose ancestors landed in Ulster three mere centuries ago from the Isle of Man; thither from France. Which part of me indeed's an Irish man?

Crippen   (*wicked*) The Popish part?

Casement   Did I become a Catholic before I died? I've some dim memory like that. Have I went religious at my end? For why?

Crippen   To swop your third class ticket for a First Class, just before your ship hit rock—

Casement   Crippen, am I doomed to lie for ever, deeved wi your felon's jibes?

Crippen   Oy oy oy then, what's the song? An English felon's cap the noblest crahn A Irish head can wear? I am wiv you alway: a puncturin voice.

Casement   (*dry*) Little I ever needed that. I had voices in me no King nor Cardinal would like to hear. But they were mine, Casement's voices, mine, all mine: the voice of Empire at my beginning, the voice of Ireland at my end; the voice that championed negro and Indian; the social charmer, the moral agitator; the voice of the Foreign Office; the voice of Sodom. All are Casement, all one man; like many bloodstreams, fuelling one discordant heart. I suffered in my dissonance but am thankful, thankful and joyous, I was on earth a while to suffer so. I go from England now, my living grave, to Ireland, land of my life; Ireland, at the exact end of this craft's trajectory: I am here, free, borne on wings to her. And at the

16

mere thought of being there again, I come alive again,
with tears . . .

(*Sounds of powerful take-off meanwhile*)

Crippen Which vein of your heart, though, akooshla makree, will
Mother Ireland want?

(*Sound of aircraft climb. Mix at ff to:*)

V

(*City gunfire, fire-sirens. Fade down*)

Author (*in small hall, his Ulster tinge slightly more marked*) Now some,
ladies and gentlemen, here in Ireland especially, would
mythologize Casement, rejecting those aspects that seem
not to fit a hero. I think we must take the whole man.
Perhaps the whole man is more a hero even, than his
Irish part.

Announceress Belfast. At a time of civil disorder, the Author addresses
a literary society there.

Author We must now consider various arguments as to whether
the Diaries so-called are genuyne or not.

(*Gunfire etc. fade discreetly to silence*)

Was Casement queer? His childhood relations establish
a classical base for homosexuality in later life. His
obsessively meticulous character, thorough almost to
retardment, fully accords with the Freudian 'anal'
personality. More concretely, Casement's counsel at his
trial, Serjeant Sullivan – I quote, was 'sick to death of
hearing Casement glory in his vice.'
Even proving Casement queer won't prove the diaries
genuine. The Diarist – let us call him that – the Diarist's
is a passive fixation. His delight is all in being at the
receiving end of other men's virility. A tall order, to
concoct a bogus journal, consistently and consummately
in tune with this one, specific, extreme, homosexual type.
Whoever wrote these diaries, experienced this fixation at
first hand.

Irish lady (*midway down hall; young, measured, inly intense*) I take it then, you accept the diaries as genuine?

Mrs Begley (*thick Belfast*) Houl' yer tongue there ahn' let the spaker spake.

Belfast student (*farther back in hall*) The forgery theory is nationalist escapism.

Irish lady (*shouting to him*) To accept how deep in filth the British will steep their hands for political ends is not escapis n—!

Belfast student Is Ireland so much the apple of God's eye, she must insist on a plaster saint for every patriot?

Irish lady (*upset*) It is not a question of plaster saints—!

Belfast student Parnell again?

Irish lady It is a matter of justice for the dead—!

Mrs Begley Sit dyne!

(*Brief pause. Distant gunfire pp*)

Author The Diaries are five. The first is a Field Service notepad, a record, most fragmentary, of Congo journeys nineteen-o-one. No scandalous entries, but much that seems psychologically illuminating, in an oblique way: newspaper cuttings and quotes, money-sums, journey-times, sketch-maps of African villages etc.

The second is a Letts' Pocket Diary for nineteen-o-three: black, size 'twelve-enlarged', roughly octavo – not quite legal size – one inch thick; printed price, four shillings. But, on the inside cover, the price 'three shillings' has been pencilled in. I infer from this that the Diarist bought this diary some way into the year. Someone who espouses the forgery theory, might of course find in this 're-maindered' price a sinister trail worth following.

Here, in nineteen-o-three, we find the first crop of those fatal homosexual references. Also, many unconscious tragic ironies and illuminations of that oblique sort I hinted at above. On the flyleaf, for instance, jotting down a French-English wordlist: for 'fourbe' the Diarist has written 'cozener'. Archaic? In England, perhaps. Shakespearian words are still current in Ulster here, they came over with Plantation.

(*Distance-muffled explosion*)

Then, March thirteenth. X. A diarist's standard symbol for a secret sexual encounter. X, Agostinho, four dollars. March seventeenth, got shamrock.

The Diarist sometimes writes House, Home with a capital H. Casement never had a permanent address. Rooms in Victoria, but he seems hardly ever there. Not even a flat of his own here in Ireland. At his trial, he was formally described as 'of no fixed abode'.

The Diarist uses occasional Ulsterisms. But rather self-consciously, in double quotes: as though phrases not fully natural to him nor proper. Years later, this same Diarist will be recording, in a special relaxed expansive hand the memory seems to invite from him, local idioms used by the lads he goes with here in Belfast. One can be drawn by a regional speech. How much more so, by the speech of the young people, from whose nationhood you feel disinherited?

January eight, nineteen-o-four, this diary breaks off. Six years follow, diaryless – without surviving diaries, that is. But, from documents, files, Casement's voluminous correspondence, the historical Casement we can, I think, theoretically reconstruct. His atrocity report on the Congo is submitted. The Foreign Office request him to tone it down: 'International good manners'. Casement is anxious to do nothing that will leave the Africans worse off than before. He rewrites the report, leaving out all names.

World reaction is one of fury: partly at the horrors the report reveals; but partly at Casement himself, whom Leopold – and the Pope – stigmatize as – I quote – 'a tool of British imperialism, hiding big business intentions behind a humanitarian smirk', 'a Protestant smearer of Mother Church' etcetera etcetera. Casement expects the Foreign Office to bear him out, but—

Casement In what high ploy has my moral passion been a pawn? Thon fella's ripped arse and torn bag is nothing to these. I see them now: 'Got to get the Belgies on the hop, what? When the rumpus dies down, pick up a few of the pieces ourselves, ha ha. By the way, that tie of yours, is it a school I ought to kneow? *Ballymena? Eoh, Eyeland!* Yes.

Lovely country, of course. Charming eccent, charming. Started up a movement in Dablin, I heah, to speak Seltic again. Who wants to speak Seltic when he can speak like us, with such a charming breogue?' (*sotto*) They are not looking at me. But through me. The English have a God, an ancestral demon, tribal, to whom my racially inferior sense can never be attuned. To these, I am profane. Must I for ever creep back from the lands of the sun to serve such sniftering effigies of men? (*Ulsterish*) Ay, hat in hand. For bread.

Author He buries his energies underground, to agitate for action in the Congo. He helps form a Congo Association, to promote the reforms governments will not. For years these activists meet, publish, circularize, plan, pronounce. All their efforts come constantly up against some indefinable brick wall, some unwritten Thou-Shalt-Not in that elusive ritual the British are for ever at in that gentlemen's madhouse of theirs across the water.

On the surface meanwhile, his career continues. But it is marked by sudden storms, rifts, sulks and sickness: consulates are offered him – Lisbon, he endures for a month then peevishly throws up: Stockholm and some French Canadian island he out of hand rejects. Malaria is taking its toll of his temper and judgment. But is the disease one of body only? He has already co-authored – anonymously, in nineteen-five – a Sinn Féin pamphlet calling on Irishmen to refuse conscription. In one last desperate attempt to please Casement, the FO offer him Haiti. Casement, delighted, turns down an alternative business offer to be free; then Haiti is appointed, to someone else. Casement's disenchantment with the Foreign Office is complete. Nineteen-o-eight, he is posted in South America.

Casement (*black, quite Ulsterish*) Ay, the mouth of the Amazon, a dump called Pará. My only consolation here is to think of the Government forking out to bury me—

Author A funeral which ultimately will happen twice, at the public expense of two different states; and might yet, as we shall see, have to be done again a third time, at the expense of a third.

From Pará, the notepaper on which Casement writes has a new letterhead, designed by himself: Consulate of Great Britain *and* Ireland. A crack in the kingdom.

January thirteenth, nineteen-ten, a Thursday: the Diarist resumes:

Diarist (*dark, slow, 'lust' voice*) X. Deep to hilt. Gabriel Ramos. Gabriel Querido. Fifteen dollars. Twenty dollars. In *very* deep thrust.

(*Fade up distant gunfire etc. meanwhile; some disturbance in hall, coughs, etc.*)

Author This nineteen-ten is a Dollard's Office Diary, printed in Dublin, roughly foolscap size. We meet a Mario, an Antonio, finally a Ramón—

Diarist (*lust voice*) Ten inches at least. *In.* Tiger!

Author Early April, the Diarist leaves for England—

Diarist Ramón for the last time. Tiger, never again.

Author April twenty-ninth, passing through—

Diarist Bay of 'Viscaya'.

Author Disdaining, presumably on political principle, to use English 'Biscay'. Next day—

Diarist (*a little Irish*) Lands End. In Irish Sea. *Saw Ireland.*

Author Underlined. Then, June six, Ballycastle: the Diarist's first entry in Gaelic. He Gaelicizes the name of a visitor, on the

[Fayzh na nglown] way to a Féis na nGleann, Festival of the Glens. July twenty:

[Sossona] Diarist Return to Sasana.

Author Sasana, Gaelic for England.

Meanwhile, the Diarist is notching up substitutes for the ten-inch tiger Ramón. There is a well-endowed young John McGonagal here in Belfast: 'huge, and he awfully kind.' Perhaps he is still alive, somewhere in this burning place. But chiefly there is 'Millar'—

Diarist (*lust voice*) Rode gloriously, splendid steed. First time after so many years, deep mutual longing.

Author His relation with Millar seems the nearest the Diarist came to abiding love.

(*More disturbance in hall*)

Voices Really! I'm not sittin' here to listen to this . . . (etc.)

21

(Sounds of people walking out)

Mrs Begley Ay, yous go!

Anglicized girl (from back of hall) There's a theory the Whitehall diaries were neither forged nor genuine.

Author Are you thinking of the theory the diary is genuine, but somebody else's?

Anglicized girl I'm thinking of two things—

Mrs Begley Spake up there, chil'!

Anglicized girl (nervous, louder, quite Irish really) When Casement later that year investigated the Portuguese cruelties in Peru, hadn't Conan Doyle asked him also to research hómósexuality amongst the tribes there?

Author It seems so. But no result of any such research, as far as I know, survives.

Anglicized girl Or could Casement, as part of his evidence for the Commission, have transcribed an obscene diary by one of the Portuguese managers he went to investigate?

Author This has been suggested. The Diarist's sexuality is all voluptuous. The Portuguese were sexuals of a different kind.

Summer nineteen-ten, the Diarist's personality – as shown in his writing – begins to fragmentate. Entries thrown in on top of each other, added piecemeal, black ink, red, thick nib and thin, heavy pencil, light. Phallic references, in an oblique round hand, relaxed, slant rightwards up across the spikier social text.

Eleventh July. Main text, scribbled, ink: the Diarist is asked to lead an investigation of a Portuguese Rubber Company's collection methods in Amazonian Peru. Left of this, neat, a line or two about developments in his Congo Reform Association. To the right, in fine nib, handwriting precise, ceremonial, controlled: details of several Foreign Office calls he pays that day. Below, slanting upwards, that fourth handwriting—

Diarist (lust voice) Carlo. But did not go.

Author Reminiscent of May that year—

Diarist (lust voice) Sent postcard to Ramón. *(English)* King's funeral service. *(Irish)* Did not go.

Author Two weeks after he arrives at Amazonmouth – en route for Peru, August – the Diarist is doodling to see how they look, various forms of a name for a nation that did not yet exist—

Diarist (*Irish*) Er-in. Er-en. Er-ie. Er-a. – Eire. *Eire*.

Author Up Amazon, the Diary becomes voluminous, spilling from page to page. Botanical observations; sketches; calculations of time and mileage, psychotically precise. Discomfort: losses at bridge – many. Interviews with witnesses, prefects, missionaries; ultimately with the Putamayo atrocity-victims themselves. Heart of Darkness indeed. Four months of this; then the Diarist returns to England, to catalogue the horror.

The Diary continues into nineteen-eleven. But first there is the Ledger. This, small, black in its half-leather binding, records – again pathological detail – every penny given to beggars, spent on matches, newspapers, public lavatories—

Diarist 'To Saint James's Palace to be knighted by King George the Fifth. Taxi and back: three shillings.'

Author Xs abound. So too, names, nicknames, pseudonyms of youths and boys; isolated exclamations:

Diarist (*lust voice*) Beauty. Enormous. Splendid. Huge.

Author Sometimes egregious measurements. In pencilled digits, tinged, he keeps a running tally with each new partner he acquires. By the beginning of August, he has noted thirty-one. One entry shows how to the pure all things are filth. The Whitehall transcript – as later published in Paris – has the Diarist pay a certain sum for a 'Grenadier'. The ledger has this clearly as a glass of Grenadine.

The Nineteen-eleven diary proper is a Letts' Desk Diary, large quarto, black. Its text – the most obscene of all – does not really get under way until late summer, when he is sent up Amazon a second time, officially to confirm his findings of the year before. And now the dam bursts: filled with a furtive desperate joy, night after night the Diarist prowling, searching his dark crude partners: encounters, yearnings; episodes in cubicles or under bushes, the Diarist serving this or that gigantic phallus tenderly with mouth or hand, or worsted and voluptuously savaged in tussles of quite brute carnality. His appetite grows as it feeds. The record has a bleakness, a radiant factual anguish, that make a literary gent like Genet look pretentious.

Through all this threads the Diarist's public voice: hobnobbing with the English colony—

Diarist (*English*) Lunch with the Pogsons. Vile grub.

Author And panicking at the delay in customs clearance for his baggages.

(*Fade up distant gunfire etc. again*)

If these are forgeries, then they add up to a fictional masterpiece of Joycean virtuosity. Through all this schizoid, kaleidoscopic multiplicity, many-personed, many-voiced, there is emerging one awareness: the shell of Sir Roger, QM, CMG, KT, being violently sloughed; the full-winged pathic-and-patriot Casement struggling obscenely to be born.

I do not seek to blacken or to vilify. If Ireland would undo the damage the British have done to Casement's name, then let her look this Casement square in the eye, and defiantly wave his sodomies at England like a flag. They are integral to Casement's triumph. And triumph, his was. I believe the Casement hanged in nineteen-sixteen had in all his born days done no living man nor woman any harm. Far from it. He had helped hoist up a little its darkness from the earth; brought hope to some of its slaves; helped bring about a measure of independence for the countrymen of his own land; and, on the way, assuaged the burgeoning sap of the randy of four continents. Not many live, who leave their fellowmen so much to thank them for. What sanity is it, ends that with a rope?

Casement's triumph, I said. What is his triumph? This. Through horror, sickness, danger, sodomy, farce, he hacks out a new definition of himself. For that, is he a hero: and not for Ireland only. For Ireland today, of course, he has a more immediate, pressing relevance: with which of us, Ireland or England, must the Ulsterman Protestant in the end throw in his Red Hand? But Casement has a relevance to all mankind. He recreates himself in terms of his own inner truth. That act, courageous, at times humiliating and absurd, transcending poetry and lust and death, makes Roger Casement a hero for the world—

(*Disturbance, screams, violent intrusion into hall. Voices shout:*

Irish voices (*shout, dangerous*) Where is the Orange bastard is slanderin our heroes? (*quiet, dangerous*) Blow out his eyes.

(*Cut. Silence*)

VI

Announceress Fragments from the Author's projected play.
A Scene. Night. The shadows of a tropical park. A young Indian, dark, stands naked, astride. In white consular jacket, shirt-tails, the bearded Casement kneels pale before him.

Casement (*sotto, a little Irish*) Black fork before me. Like a fork in a night road. One way, to a knighthood, a peerage: to end embalmed, more English than the English themselves. But where the other way . . . ?
Black fork, black monkeyfork of an Indian lad, black thighs astride, his proud yard up – black as the Earl of Hell's waistcoat, hard as iron, thick as a wrist: oh, shovel thon intill me deep, deep . . .
No bush much on him, to speak of. But good wine needs no bush—

Announceress A policeman goes by, beyond the trees.

Casement Sh—

Indian (*laughs*)

Announceress But the Indian merely laughs, and suddenly thrusts Casement down and over. The bodies jerk; then slowly rock, white horse, black rider covering him.

Casement (*sotto*) Savage, so-called. Me, civilizationer, so-called. Savage has life, pink Christian pig has only things . . . Pink Christian pigs possess; the savage *is* . . . This giant lives and moves to be; I toil and die to have . . .
Another road . . . Thon other road . . . Away from

England: sucked down, down, down deep in mire . . .
and milk and blood . . . Like happens till Ireland's
conquerors in time, that mount her, grab handhold on
her sides and shores. Absorption, down, down intill her
mire and blood . . .

(*Silence*)

I, Casement, Ulster's Red Hand, last stranger tissue to
invade her flesh not yet absorbed . . . now I dissolve upon
an emerald field . . .

Announceress The Indian comes away. Casement sinks.

Casement Fork fork . . . Which way for me? One way, museum lies.
But this road, what?

(*Pause*)

Announceress Fragments from the author's projected play.
Two complementary scenes.
A. The man that Casement could have, but did not,
become. Lord Ballycastle, now doyen of British diplomats
and very-old, gives interview on the eve of publication
of his memoirs, The Red Hand Serves the Craown.

Joan Bakewell Lord Ballycastle. I would like to ask you, if I may, to cast
your mind back to the summer of nineteen-ten.

Casement (*husky, very elderly, somewhat Livesey-like*) Ah. Putamayo.

Joan Bakewell According to your book, the Putamayo were a remote
tribe of the Upper Amazon, under Peruvian government,
who were being pressed into labour by a Portuguese
Rubber Company, the Arana, based in London.

Casement Quite so, yes.

Joan Bakewell What legal authority did the British Government have, to
conduct an investigation?

Casement Some blacks of ours, Barbadians mainly, were wandering
in from neighbouring British protectorates. Nasty
rumours of brutality were filtering through to the FO.

Joan Bakewell You describe your journey up the Amazon as most
uncomfortable.

Casement The river stank, the steamer was stuffy, the crew in-
competent. Mosquitoes, equatorial downpour, thunder
most of the time. Appalling. Reached my consulate at the
end of August.

Joan Bakewell That – that's the town, Iquitos.

Casement Iquitos, yes.

Joan Bakewell Well, m —

Casement Dirty hole. Indians everywhere, crawling with soldiers in the slovenliest blue uniforms – fine specimens, but abominable.

Joan Bakewell You made some interesting philosophical observations about this time.

Casement Yes.

(Silence)

Joan Bakewell For instance – I quote: The man who gives up his family, his nation, his language, is worse than the woman who abandons her virtue. What chastity is to her, self-respect and self-knowledge are to manhood. Men are conquered, not by invaders, but by their own moral turpitude.

Casement I stand by that.

Joan Bakewell Er, – Having established your base at Iquitos, you continued up river.

Casement It began to become apparent that the stories were true. At one place, La Chorerra I think it was, young Indians showed us their buttocks: devastatingly slashed from flogging. Tapir-hide. The overseers jollied us along: one of them even made a fourth at bridge. Offhandedly confessed he had beheaded five Indians himself. Felt I was going a slam in spades with the devil doubling, ha ha. And Jimenez, I remember, nasty, half-caste, nasty, had the gall to dine with us. Ha ha, when he saw us off, he was waving his cap. I remember saying to Barnes, Pity we can't wave his head.

Joan Bakewell And so you go on, to the heart of the horror. On October the seventeenth, you came into the territory of Armando Normand.

Casement Yes. He turned up surrounded by a harem of native concubines. I would not have taken to him, even if I had not known he had recently baked two little Indian boys alive on a hob; the skin peeled off them while they were still screaming, a soldier had to shoot them to end their agony. He was a monster. He had a habit of soaking men and women in kerosene and setting light to them. He burnt them at the stake. He dashed out children's brains. He cut off Indians' legs and arms and left them to die. He put some in the stocks to starve to death, eating the maggots from their own wounds. The man was mad.

Joan Bakewell It may seem a foolish question, Lord Ballycastle, but, why did the Indians put up with this? Surely, in their own jungle—

Casement Ah, but there the Spaniards and Portuguese were very clever, you see. They got men of one tribe to kidnap slaves from another: then there would be a 'backlash', the survivors in the kidnapped tribe would massacre the raiders; then there would be reprisals. The Portuguese simply exploited local hatreds, to harvest the rubber. My God, those Latins in America have got a lot to answer for.

Joan Bakewell But in treating their labour force so destructively weren't they in effect killing the goose that laid their golden eggs?

Casement The Arana weren't interested in *developing* the Putamayo. They were only there to pillage and get out. The Indians would last them just as long as the rubber did. I think the Portuguese had calculated that.

Joan Bakewell How did the Foreign Office react to your report?

Casement They asked me to tone it down, of course. In earlier days I would have hit the roof at that, but, ha, I was an old hand now, I was learning to work on the principle, ask for the stars if you want only the moon. Besides, however I respectabilized the language, the tale itself was horrible enough.

Joan Bakewell And how did the world react?

Casement Scandalized. *The Times* gave me two columns and an editorial. White House brought pressure. But who were US to call the kettle black? Nine thousand negroes had been lynched there during nineteen-o-nine alone. Besides, US were under the spell of the Monroe doctrine at that time.

Joan Bakewell Oh, that the Western Hemisphere belongs to Washington.

Casement Mm.

Joan Bakewell Mm. Finally, Lord Ballycastle, do you regard your expedition as a success?

Casement What do you mean by 'success'? Personally it was: I got my knighthood for it, and that was the basis of all my subsequent career. As far as the Indians were concerned, it was not a success. My revelations forced the Arana into liquidation, and that left the whole area exposed to any racketeer who could muster enough staff to pick up what was left. I intervened personally with President Taft – on some boat, I remember. I tried to persuade Carnegie to finance a more humanitarian company. I almost succeeded in establishing a Christian mission in the area – but that came to nothing when the Protestants and Catholics started quarrelling over who should run it. The Peruvian Government played a waiting game; which came off. Within a year or two, the Great War had broken out. By nineteen-eighteen the Putamayo Indian was extinct. But for my memoirs, no one today would even know their name.

Joan Bakewell Lord Ballycastle, thank you.

(*Pause*)

Announceress Fragment, complementary to the above. Scene B: the reoad he did take. To the reope.

(*Fade up faintest thunder of wavebreak on rocks, subtly maintain throughout*)

The Northeast coast of Eyeland. Murlock Bay. Casement, in an Aran sweater, walks sleowly, peryusing a little green book that has come to him that morning through the peost.

Casement (*soft Ulster voice*) 'First Steps in Irish': by Father Eugene OGrowney, Gaelic League, Dublin. Atá mé, I am. Atá

[Recommended Gaelic League pronunciation of the time: *athaw*may, thoo, shay, shee, shin, shiv, *shee*adh. Fane.]

tú, you are. Atá sé, atá sí, he is, she is. Atá sinn, we are, atá sibh, yous are, atá siad, they are. Emphatic Particle: féin. Mé féin, me, emphatic. Sé féin, sí féin, him, her: emphatic. Sinn – féin . . .

Glorious one, green eyes, at corner of Donegall Street waiting for Crumlin Road tram. He saw me. Longed, I could tell . . .

The Noun. 'As in Latin, the Irish noun changes its ending to denote function in the sentence. Sometimes a suffix is added; sometimes a final vowel changed between shallow and deep. The Irish noun, however, can also mutate at its beginning: sometimes by aspiration or breathing – e.g. Séumas, James. To form the Vocative Case, aspirate the initial S and bring forward the deep vowel at its end: Séumas; oh James, a Shéumais . . .'

[Shaymus]

[A haymish]

Young Jamie MacAllister's is growin nicely. In Ormeau Park with him, a day in May, a glorious day. I take it up for him, fully eight inches he has at extension, and the red head of it huge. 'Boys, but that's grand,' he whispers; 'thon's grand . . .'

Where is my speech? Was it ever my speech? I – am – unvoiced . . . Three times an exile. Irishman in England. Ulsterman in Ireland. Queer in the world . . .

'The Perfect Tense. Irish has no direct way of inflecting its verbs to denote past action. We do not say "We lost that battle" but "That battle is lost for us", usually Anglicised as "We are after losing" etcetera. "It is had at me": "I am after having" . . .'

How many lads are after having me this year so far? Denis, Pierre . . . Fred, Ernest, Fanti . . . Five. The Yid, Welsh Rarebit, Laurens of West India Docks; Lofty . . . Jock of Sloane Square . . . Ahmon, 'Karl' at the Ritz, Pasto . . . 'Friend' of Belfast: 'Like it rightly' . . . Seventeen, eighteen . . . Ballymena baths: fair hair, eyes blue, rippling bodies brown and swift, beautiful Irish young men, the glorious boys of Erin, big and fair . . .

June seven, lavatory one d, bus two d, train five d, tea four d, twelve copies of *Truth* one shilling, five *Daily News* threep'nce, paper one d, cigarettes sixpence, copy of *Sinn Féin* one d . . . June fifteen: letter from Sir Edward Grey telling of knighthood. Alack! Then Uxbridge, lovely boy scout and Chaney's baker lad . . .

'The Copula. Irish distinguishes two separate aspects of the verb To Be. One. To describe a subject, e.g. The day is cold, the verb atá is used. Two. To make a statement of identity, e.g. It is a book, the Copula is is used.'

[iss]

Atá mé, atá mé; say of Casement something not by nature true. Consul. CMG, KT . . . 1s. 1s. Say of me something I inly, by my own definition, am . . .

(Wavebreak faded meanwhile. Soon:)

VII

(Colossal gongstroke. Let vibrate)

Crier Oyez! Oyez! Give eah! Give eah to me! The English civilize Eyeland: a panorama of 'istoree!

England *(elderly, port-slurred)* Be fair now, be fair now, be objective, be fair.

(Primordial wind-moan, bleak, low. Slow pendulum-swing, a pulse of time. Two commentators, man, woman, 'World at One' style, objectively alternate:)

She Ireland. The dawn of time. Waves of westward migration across Asia and Europe must all end here, the known world's edge. Each oncoming race can do one of only two things: be driven underground in turn by those that follow; or, stand, back to the ocean, face and absorb them. Four thousand BC, putative date of first fortification of Armagh.

He At some pre-Christian stage a northern Kingdom Ulster reaches south as far as the river Boyne. Other kingdoms of Ireland unite in coalition. North-south strife reflected in legends of a Great Wall of Ulster, the Black Pig Dyke. Also, at turn of the age BC–AD, in Gaelic epic poem, the Quest for the Bull.

She The Queen of the West, taking no pride in the prize White Bull of her consort, covets the Brown Bull of the North. Leads her southern allies in a raid to capture it.

[Cahoolan] Are defeated by Northern hero Cú Chúllain, but seize Brown Bull as trophy, bring it west. Brown Bull and White set on each other, pursue and harry each other to death; all Ireland covered with their bleeding remains.

He The hundreds AD: kingdoms of Ireland loosely ally into roughly equal northern and southern federations. Soon, a dyarchy: Crown of All Ireland passing alternately north and south. Religion Druidic.

She Third century: olympiads and royal parliaments established on Hill of Tara.

He Fourth century, fifth: Roman Empire rots at fringe, Gaels encroach inward. Some invade Alban, rename it Scot-land after themselves.

31

Casement The Scots are only Irish who learnt how to swim.

She Shut up Casement, back in your box.
Christianization of Ireland. Four-thirty-two AD, Patrick –
or another of the same name – lands, converts Druid
High King, establishes archbishopric of Armagh four-
forty-five.

He Irish Church develops monastic rather than dogmatic
tradition; persists for seven centuries in certain hetero-
doxies at variance with Rome.

She Six century, seventh: darkness in Europe. Ireland alone,
offshore, remote, is safe. University of Armagh, one of its
most famous alumni Alfred the Great. An Irish Abbot
preaches that the earth is a sphere. Books of Durrow,
Kells.

He Seven-nine-five: Viking raids on Irish north-east coast.
Sack of Armagh. Vikings found Dublin eight-four-one.
Later also Wicklow, Wexford, Waterford.

She Gaels assimilate the Danes. North-south dyarchy dis-
integrates. Vandalism, tribal war.

He Nine-seven-six: a western prince Brian Boroimhe

[Baroo] usurps his way to kinghood paramount. Selfstyled
Imperator Scotorum, re-establishes city and sanctuary of
Armagh, royal glory of Tara. His divorced wife calls
non-assimilated Danes to ally with Danes from England
to depose him.

She Battle of Clontarf, Good Friday, ten-fourteen: Boroimhe
drives the invading Danes back into sea; is killed. Ireland
fragmentates again.

He The Romanization of Ireland. Eleven-forty, Malachi of
Armagh begins reform of dogma and ritual of Irish
Church, into line with Rome. Eleven-fifty-one, King
Dermot of Leinster abducts wife of a neighbouring
King, then flees to Henry the Second of England
for help. Eleven-fifty-five, Englishman Pope Hadrian
the Fourth authorizes Henry of England to complete
Romanization of Irish Church. Eleven-seventy, Anglo-
Normans invade.

Crier The English in Eyeland, a 'istoree—!

England (*as before*) Be fair, now. Both sides of the story, be fair. Be
objective, be fair . . .

She Eleven-seventy-one. Victorious Henry summons Irish princes to do him homage. High King, also Chiefs of Ulster, refuse. All others obey. Newly Orthodoxized hierarchy acknowledge Henry as rightful King of Ireland.

He Irish and Irishized Danes now merging absorb Normans also. Irishized Normans drift apart from Anglo-Norman Establishment in Dublin Garrison.

She Statutes of Kilkenny, thirteen-sixty-seven. Native law of Ireland dislegitimized. Intermarriage, wearing of Irish dress, speaking of Irish made punishable by death.

He Anglo-Norman colony set up military enclosure, the Pale, to protect shrinking Dublin-centred enclave from Irish and Irishized Normans and Danes increasingly ungovernable beyond. Fourteen-eighty-seven, Tudor reconquest of Ireland: Sir Edward Poynings Lord Deputy. A new repression begins. Fifteen-thirty-four, revolt led by GaeloNorman FitzGerald dynasty savagely crushed. Plantation—

She
[Leesh] Inaugurated by Catholic Mary Tudor. Renames counties Laois and Offaly Queen's and King's County after herself and Philip of Spain. Fifteen-eighty: England reProtestantized, GaeloNormans again rebel. Spanish Brigade lands on Kerry coast. Perrott: bastard halfbrother of Good Queen Bess, fires crops, slaughters cattle. Famine. Submission.

Crier New Irish estates available for rightminded English gentlemen!

[Rawley] *She* Beneficiaries include Sir Walter Ralegh; Edmund Spenser, author of the 'Faerie Queen'.

He Sporadic trouble meanwhile from the North: raspberries blown at Limey Liz by succession of maverick princes O Neill of Tyrone. Queen Bess—

Bess (*virago*) Inseminate the North!

He And James the First—

James I (*Scot*) Inseminate the Norrth!

She Northern farmlands confiscated: trumped-up charges, intimidation of juries. Warwickshire, Kent farmers uprooted, deported to pastures of Armagh and Down. Ulster's dispossessed driven to the high ground. City of

Derry made over to group of London speculators, its name symbolically demoted to a suffix, later a loose-jawed sneer in English mouths—

England London-dreh.

He Sixteen-forties. Ireland between hammer of Protestant Parliament and anvil of divine-right monarchy. Charles the First seeks to manipulate Irish dispossessed against pro-Parliament Plantationer families who now again have everything to lose. Situation complicated by influx, into north and south-east, of Protestant and Dissenter refugees from Britain and pogroms of Catholic Europe. Trails of sectarian gunpowder begin to flare: e.g. Sligo sixteen-forty-two, Protestant couples trussed in coital postures and burnt alive.

She Charles' bid to mobilize Ireland against Parliament fails. Sixteen-forty-nine, January, Charles beheaded. September, Cromwell embarks on Final Solution.

He Barns filled with Irish prisoners and set alight. Children rolled downhill in barrels studded with nails. Cats tied together by tails, slung over rope to fight to the death in Kilkenny streets. Churches desecrated. Populations of Drogheda and Wexford wiped out.

Cromwell (*utterly sincere*) It has pleased God to bless our endeavours in this town this day: we put to the sword the whole number. I wish that all honest hearts may give the glory of this to God alone, to Whom indeed the praise of this mercy belongs.

England We will not negotiate with thugs and murderers.

Englishwoman I don't like what he did to those cats at all.

She Cromwell's Settlement. Women and children to slavery in the Indies. Survivors driven west to barren regions of bog or stone—

Cromwell To Hell or Conn-nought!

He Lands reallocated to soldiers, new plantationers. Some soldiers cannot settle, take to life of banditry, terrorism, preying on all alike: soon to acquire a nickname, Tories. Andrew Marvell—

Marvell   And now the Irish are ashamed
        To find themselves in one year tamed—

She Sixteen-sixty, Monarchy restored. Irish trades that

threaten English counterparts – e.g. cattle, wool – subjected to prohibitive dues, systematically destroyed.

England I always said the Irish were a drain on our economy.

Englishwoman But at least it saved your lovely countryside. You might have been like Bradford otherwise. Ireland is a lovely place for a holiday now.

England And to retire to. No crime.

Englishwoman And none of those filthy plays.

He Sixteen-eighty-seven, James the Second attempts a restitution of native Irish rights. Deposed. Replaced by bisexual Dutchman, William of Orange. Ireland now a critical hinge in European Prot-Cat power game. Cats land in Ireland, backed by Louis Quatorze; establish springboard for restoration of Cat monarchy in England. Their advance, only the city of Derry resists, where thirteen Protestant apprentice boys take law into own hands, slam gates in Jacobite army's face. Siege of Derry begins.

She Schomberg lands with Huguenots, William of Orange with Dutch and German mercenaries – backed by the Pope, who wants to cut the Sun King down to size. Derry relieved, Jacobite carpet rolled back. Sixteen-ninety, July the Twelfth: James and William meet at Battle of River Boyne. James routed, earns undying nickname *Séumas an Chaca*, James the Shite.

[Shaymus un Khocka]

James II (*breathless*) O woman, woman of the house, my army have all run away.

Irishwoman Ay, an' your Majesty has bate them in the race.

He Protestant revenge. Remnants of Irish military caste dispersed abroad – Flight of the Wild Geese, so-called: Irish surnames henceforth pepper armylists of France Spain Russia Hungary. Treaty of Limerick: guarantees the vanquished Irish equality of rights. Penal Laws follow. No Irish Catholic may buy land, rent land, inherit land. Priesthood outlawed. Legal definition of an Irish Catholic: animal with no official existence. Anglicanism at a premium: elsewhere beyond the Pale, widespread starvation. Anglican Dean of a Dublin cathedral proposes satirically that Irish children be reared for pork. Catholic

Irish identity adopts new tactic to survive: goes underground.

(Hallelujah Chorus breaks out ff:)

Crier Oyez, oyez! Queen Anne is dead! Krauts get their mits on the English crahn!

She Scotland meanwhile, story much the same. Nazi methods of 'Herzog von Kumberlant', with Swiss and Austrian mercenaries, and help of traditional turncoat highlanders of Argyll, combine with Bonnie Prince Charlie's tactical incompetence to finish Scottish Gaeldom for ever: February, the thirteenth, seventeen-forty-six, Culloden Moor.

He Belfast founded. Dublin, Handel's 'Messiah', world première.

She Ireland now an imperial colony, Dublin a grand viceregal capital. Anglican patronage, plutocracy, a pocket parliament. Now Dissenter, refugee, plantationer stock awaken to their own disfranchisement. Age of Reason: Tom Paine, Voltaire. French and American republicanism in the air; similar political ideas published from Belfast by Protestant republican Wolfe Tone. Are Ireland's grievances a potential revolutionary seedbed on England's doorstep? Anglican enlightenment and self-interest coincide: Penal Laws rescinded; an 'independent' Dublin Parliament set up.

He But this proves a reactionary garrison-minded junta, and is not accountable to any electorate. Catholic and Dissenter beyond the pale begin to sense a common cause: 'Wolfe Tone' movement for a United Irish secular Republic.

Hierarchies and Establishment combine.

An unholy trinity Divide, and rule! Inflame the North!

He Ulster, seventeen-nineties: medieval religious hatreds 'mysteriously' revive. Orange Order: identifying Protestantism with British loyalty. Opposing terror-groups spring up, sectarian mayhem prevails. United Irish movement fails, Tone goes to Revolutionary France to prepare more violent means. An Irish rebellion begins to ignite, the authorities move—

Unholy trinity First pacify the North!

    She Dublin garrison unleash on Ulster an unprincipled and disciplineless militia, to liquidate dissenters and political unreliables there. Only after two generals have on principle refused to mastermind this holocaust is the command accepted, by a General Lake.

    He Rebellion thus mainly confined to Huguenot and Catholic peasantry, parish priests of South-East. Rebel pikelads gather 'at the rising of the moon': the Ninety-Eight. British Army has many loyal Irish Catholic soldiers in its ranks. Traditional punishment for rebel prisoners, a cap of burning pitch.

    She Prime Minister Pitt gets the message–

    Pitt Ireland must never, never, never again be left at liberty to foster ideas and aspirations inimical to the British way of life.

    She The hierarchies concur. For a million pounds in bribe and indemnity, Dublin Parliament agrees to its own dissolution. Act of Union, eighteen-o-one: the Jack acquires Saint Patrick's Cross. Pitt sees, what his less farsighted colleagues do not–

    Pitt The surest instrument of British dominance in Ireland will be the hierarchy of the Catholic Church.

    She And symbolically endows the seminary of Maynooth.

    He Industrial Revolution. England must be independent of Europe for her food. Ireland's new rôle–

    England Kitchen-garden for our increased industrial prosperity.

    He Her native industries diseconomized. Industrial employment falls to one tenth in twenty years. The Irish driven back to the land. But enclosures, clearances. Landlords forcibly expand and dispopulate their Irish estates. Countryside fills with starving and dispossessed. To keep these in order, eighteen-fifteen, a Constabulary founded by Sir Robert Peel: the RIC.

    She Eighteen-seventeen, famine. Eighteen-twenty-one, famine. Irish habeas corpus suspended, right of assembly annulled. Daniel O Connell: monarchist conservative Gael from Kerry, establishes power base among peasantry and parish clergy. Three aims: end religious discrimination; reform land-ownership system; ultimate self-government.

Eighteen-twenty-eight, O Connell elected for County Clare. Election declared void. O Connell re-elected. Property qualification for vote steeply raised, two pounds to ten. O Connell's Emancipation Bill earns voice in Parliament for Catholic middle class.

He Growth of Young Ireland Party, who press O Connell too fast for his liking to move repeal of Union. Defeated. Mass rally eighteen forty-three on site of Boroimhe's victory at Clontarf, cancelled by O Connell after pressure by Peel, now PM, and Home Secretary Graham. O Connell soon fades from Irish politics.

She Eighteen-forty-five, potato famine. Forty-six, potato famine. Forty-seven, potato famine. Population of Ireland falls by two million in five years; within fifty, will be almost halved. Yet in one famine year alone, twenty million pounds' worth of foodstuff forcibly exported for English use. Scenic Antrim Coast Road built as relief. Queen Victoria contributes to famine fund.

He Eighteen-forty-eight, revolutions in Europe. A soldier
[*Coe*shoot] called Casement helps Kóssuth against the Austrians in Hungary. Young Ireland rebellion suppressed, ringleaders deported to Australia, Tasmania. Famine-ruined Irish estates bought up by middle-class speculators. Evictions. Emigration. Eighteen-fifty, formation of a land league: three aims – fair rent, fixed tenure, free sale. Eighteen-fifty-eight, formation of Irish Revolutionary Brotherhood. Eighteen-sixty-four, birth of a son to the soldier Casement: Roger David.

She Eighteen-sixty-seven: rising led by Irish Revolutionary Brotherhood. Catholic hierarchy condemn. Two years later Gladstone begins long endeavour to make amends: disestablishes the Church of Ireland.

He Eighteen-seventy-nine, potato famine. Protestant landlord Charles Parnell MP: identifies with a reconstituted Land League: fair rent, fixed tenure, free sale. His skilled manoeuvres in Parliament transform hitherto puppet Irish Party into formidable political tool, holding balance of power between Tory and Whig.

She The Irish began to hit back at their Anglo-Irish, Irish and English landlords. Tenants of a Mayo estate adopt a new technique: silent non-cooperation. Landlord's agent driven to flight, leaving only his name – Captain Boycott. Catholic hierarchy try to have Land League suppressed.

He Gladstone grants Fair Rent, Fixed Tenure, Free Sale: eighteen-eighty-one. James Joyce born. Gladstone and Parnell ally. Draft of first Irish Home Rule Bill, eighteen-eighty-six. Tories in a flutter—

Tories Oh what shall we do? What shall we do? How shall we split the Parnell–Gladstone axis? What shall we do?

She Answer. Implicate Parnell in a recent assassination in Dublin's Phoenix Park.

He But documents prove forged. Try again.

Tories We must smash the Liberals. What shall we do? – I have an idea. It worked before. – What? what? – *Inflame the North!* – Hooray, hooray: inflame the North!

She Lord Randolph Churchill visits Belfast.

Churchill Home Rule Rome Rule! No surrendah! Not an inch! Remembah the spirit of Londondreh! Ulstah will feight, and Ulstah will be reight!

She Gladstone's first Home Rule Bill defeated, his government falls. Anti-Home Rule Liberals cross House: Unionist Party born. Tories in power: new repression in Ireland. Ambitious Dublin barrister Carson—

He Remember the name—

She Crown Prosecutor there. Eighteen-eighty-nine, Parnell cited in divorce: public orgy of morality. Fall of Parnell, his death in disgrace.

He Eighteen-ninety two, Gladstone returned. Second Home Rule Bill. Commons pass. But in Lords–

Lords I say, I say, which way do we have to go? To defeat the Home Rule Bill, through which door? – Follow Lord Randolph.

He Defeated.

She Foundation in Dublin of Gaelic League. Renaissance in Irish and Anglo-Irish literature. Eighteen-ninety-six, barrister Carson—

He Remember the name—

She – prosecutes at trial of Oscar Wilde. Irish national movement begins to split. A compromise 'dominion-status' group, Home Rulers. An all-out independence group, Sinn Féin.

He Nineteen-o-six, a Captain Craig—

She Remember the name—

He —elected Unionist MP for East Down. A barrister Frederick Edwin Smith—

She Remember the name—

He —returned for a constituency in Liverpool. Première in Dublin, 'Playboy of the Western World'.

She Nineteen-o-eight, Liberal PM Asquith: officially committed to Home Rule, but threatened by ascendant Tory Carson wielding his Orange Ace. Lord Randolph's son Winston crosses House, joins Liberals: pro Home Rule. Carson—

Carson (*sneer*) That Winston will never be the sort of man the public trust.

She Wind of a third Home Rule Bill, nineteen-ten. Carson and MP Craig tour the North—

Carson, Craig Heome Rule, Reome Rule! No surrendah! Not an inch! A loyal Ulstah! God Save the King!

He Carsonites forcibly prevent Winston from addressing Home Rule meeting in Ulster Hall, Belfast. Dockers pelt him back on to his boat with rotten fish. Home Rule Bill goes into committee. Craig, Carson and Frederick Edwin Smith prepare Ulster Covenant, envisaging UDI for a Protestant Ulster. Half a million sign this, many in their own blood. Illegal army formed, Ulster Volunteers, to resist implementation of Home Rule. With an escort armed with wooden rifles, Carson parades Belfast behind a dummy cannon.

She He is now a Privy Councillor. Roger Casement knighted for services in Putamayo.

He Nineteen-thirteen, Dublin General Strike, suppressed. Irish Citizen Army formed, to protect Dublin workers against Dublin Police.

She June, Casement resigns from Foreign Office.

He Carson visits Germany, negotiating for German arms—

Carson To blow Home Rule off the English statute book with powder! The Protestants of Ireland will welcome their continental deliverer as did their fathers King William once before. God save the Kaiser!

She Gun-running into Ulster begins: Carson still Privy Councillor. October: Casement's formal début in Irish politics, a speech at Ballymoney, county Antrim – stance, anti-Carson, Protestant for independent united Ireland. November, made treasurer of Dublin-based rebel Volunteers, responsible for raising arms and funds abroad.

He London bans further imports of arms into Ireland as seditious. Carson Volunteers – now one hundred thousand strong, their funds one million pounds – land, April nineteen fourteen, forty thousand German Mausers near Belfast. Asquith squeals:

Asquith (*squeals*) An unprecedented outrage!

He Carson remains Privy Councillor.

She Southern anti-Carson Volunteers attempt similar arms-landing near Dublin during the summer. Military sent in. Shootings, deaths. Casement leaves to raise funds among Irish in America. August the fourth, World War.

Casement (*Irish*) I told Roosevelt, I told him: England will win this, then God help Ireland. Roosevelt grinned. England cannot win, he said; she's finished. I said, Roosevelt you are wrong: she will envenom America with her own imperialist disease, and join her in the plunder of the earth.

She September, Casement publicly declares–

Casement If Ireland fights for England now, it will be a gratuitous gift of her last blood in a rotten cause!

She October, Casement in Germany, see scene below.

He April twenty-first nineteen-sixteen, Good Friday, Casement lands on Kerry coast with fruit of German mission, see scene below. Arrested, taken to London.

She Monday April twenty-fourth nineteen-sixteen: Dublin insurrection. Convinced that only a blood-sacrifice will inspire the Irish nation to a general revolt, and on supposition that Englishmen will bombard anything and anybody except grand public buildings, an extremist core of seven rebel leaders seize Dublin GPO. Proclaim

Independence. After three days, General Maxwell arrives, to 'teach Ireland a lesson'.

(*Cut in 'Land of Hope and Glory' tune from Elgar Pomp and Circumstance March Number One, its grandest appearance. Very soon fade, under:*)

He Statistics of Dublin Rising. Killed. Insurgents, sixty-four. English and Irish soldiery, one hundred and thirty-four. Civilians, two hundred. Wounded, two thousand six hundred and fifteen. Arrested, three thousand five hundred and twenty-nine. Many on their way to prison mocked at, spat on, stoned by Dublin populace. Sentences. To six months imprisonment, four persons. To a year, seventeen. Two years' hard, two persons. Three years imprisonment, fifty-six. Five years, eighteen. Seven years, one. Eight years, three. Ten years, thirty-three. Twenty years, one. Life, ten. Thomas J. Clarke, for signing Declaration of Independence, death. James Connolly, for signing Declaration of Independence, death. Eamonn Ceannt, as above, death. Seán MacDiarmada, as above, death. Thomas MacDonagh, as above, death. Padraig Pearse, as above, death. Joseph Plunkett, as above, death. For parts played in the Rising: Cornelius Colbert, death; Edward Daly, death; J. J. Heuston, death; John MacBride, death; Michael Mallin, death; Michael O Hanrahan death; William Pearse, death . . .

(*Fade up meanwhile Elgar Coda. Its penultimate tutti chord is combined with a sharp unison deathshot sound. Its final chord is not heard at all: a second deathshot replaces it precisely. Thirteen further deathshots follow, spaced, grim, their intervening silences irregular and uncompromised. Then long silence. At last:*)

England Very one-sided account and selective. He didn't say anything of the good we did them. I demand the right to reply.
   Ireland Like to say what?

(*Silence*)

42

VIII

(*Tighten, as through unsettled air, toward drone of airborne craft. Wind-buffets lash, thinly whine*)

(*Inside aircraft. Drone muted. Drone of priest-voice, brief fragment of harp and woman, fading down*)

Crippen   Hey. Oy. Fruity. Casement. There's someone here wants to speak with you.

Casement   (*stage Ulster*) Who now?

Crippen   Bird. Wants an exclusive on your return to Eyeland.

Announceress   I'm sorry. Sir Roger, I thought I–

Casement   (*wild*) *Sir* Roger? *Sir?!*

Announceress   You were stripped of your knighthood, I kneow, but I thought–

Casement   After all this time, even now–?

Announceress   I didn't quite kneow how to address you; I thought, out of respect–

Casement   The Queen's Medal for South Africa I never wore. When they made me CMG I pleaded absence from the investiture with an attack of piles. Was it not plain enough after Putamayo I wanted no truck more with titles from the King of Beasts?

Announceress   Why did you accept the knighthood then?

Casement   News of it was published before I was officially informed. Had they approached me previously – as I believe is now the practice – I could have quietly refused. The premature announcement had me trapped.

Announceress   But your letter of acceptance is so fulsome–

Casement   Couched in terms as oleaginous as I could muster. The cold satiric spirit in which I phrased those thanks was something neither my ultimate prosecutors were equipped to conceive nor my biographers to hit on.

Announceress   In Germany later you wrote a letter to the Kaiser on his birthday: it is very similar.

Casement   An arselick, pure and simple. Also, my judgment was not at its strongest at that time. You're forgetting, I was trained in your Establishment. There, if we learn nothing else, we at least acquire early the knack of experiencing our insincere emotions precisely as we mouth them.

43

Announceress I take it then, at the time of your knighthood, your extremist feeling was already far advanced?

Casement How do you mean, 'extremist'?

Announceress Well – anti-English.

(*Pause*)

After all, you had begun so promisingly! What happened to change your attitude, was it some tropical disease?

Casement (*hint of Diarist's lust voice*) The black lad covered me, mounted me, biting my shoulders, my arms, my neck; with such force stove my after end, reamed, raking me, I lost my breath. I saw in that moment, out of English arseholes the sun does after all not shine. I squinied up from below that shovelling throbbing mountain of a man, and saw, like in a flare in the gallery of the sky, a vision of the English in the gods. I saw them clear. The Lord's own gift to the world. I saw then that coven of thugs in evening gowns and tails as my more honourable predecessors in the dock had seen them: a people barren of all conscience, faith or truth; enveloped in a panoplied pharisaicism and incurable hypocrisy; that pray to Christ and worship Mammon; profess liberty, and prostitute all principle to the sacred interests of the landlord class; and raise all their most successful gangsters to be peers, so to preserve the succession of false doctrine, and hand on down to their chinless sons the booty intact.

Announceress Oh come come come, one must have breeding.

Casement For why? are yous horses? Inbreed in men, the strain degenerates. (*English*) One must have a first-class team, *of course*, to bring home from the championships of the world the glorious rugger-cup of Life. (*Irish*) From that, in the nick of time, I saved myself. Down, down my lusting took me, intill a secret undergrowth deep deep beyond the pierce of social light. There are black sacraments there, blaspheme thon eggshell yous lot call the 'bedrock of societeh'; a sacred misrule, shows up the rotten fiction of all law; an emancipation of excrement and disgust, illumes with a lovely filthy gold the poison-violence of all 'moraliteh'.

Casement the sod, Casement the Pat: twin fruit of the one

44

dark juicy tree. And I went down to Dublin so, shedding like a snake its slough my English shell, committing myself with open eyes to the ecstasy and danger of my newborn forbidden selves. False steps I made, and many, on my road to tomorrow; marching out, now in whimsy, now in rage, nurturing now twee fancies of an antic Erin Gaelicly reborn, now prophetic designs for an Ireland dragged up on to the world's wide stage; I, Casement, stepping, preposterous and magnificent by turns, across that most treacherous bog our Irish topography affords, her politics; making down south through the Gap o' the North, for Drogheda, Dublin, the green-white-and-orange tricolour in my one hand, a Belfast lad's cock in the other. Ireland, I, Antrim Dissenter, will at last be yours. So to my death.

So leave me in peace to lie now, in that one place I explicitly wished, the churchyard by Antrim's Murlough Bay, my nearest ever to a home. For my epitaph, have wit and honesty enough to write: Here Casement lies, an Ulster Prot who faced the petrifying Gorgon of his split national self, and lived; and chose; the white lily of whose patriotism grew out of his backside.

(*Harp and woman, dim*)

Crippen Hey. Hey. Hey. Miss. If Fruity wants to be buried in Antrim, that's the North, i'n't it?

Announceress Sh, Crippen, please—

Crippen We ought to be on a plane for Belfast not Dublin. Hey, Fruity, Casement, wake up again, we're on the wrong bleeding plane-

Announceress Quiet! Please! We can't bury Casement in Antrim, that's Northern Eyeland, part of the UK: it would be most impolitic. He's going to Dublin: Glahsneevin, a plot marked out for him by his sister forty years ago. We'll have to hope he doesn't notice.

(*Fade plane-drone, priest-voice. End of Part One*)

IX

(German military band passes down street)

German Announceress *(accent moderately fractured)* Tchermany. October nineteen-fourteen. Berlin. Imperial Foreign Office, Wilhelmstrasse seventy-six. Office of von Wedel, Chief Secretary of English Department. Casement waits.

Casement *(Irish)* So here I sit. At the fountainhead of German policy. Am I afeared? No. I have regrets, may be, but I am not afeared. This blow I strike for Ireland today must change the course of British policy for ever; and Ireland be lifted from the parish mud, up, on the stages of the world. That at least I shall have achieved.

Wedel *(accent impeccable)* So, Sir Roger: how is America?

Casement I have to confess this damnable English War has put a spoke in all my wheels there.

Wedel They were turning?

Casement They would have begun to, given time. But at least myself and my New York colleagues are agreed, how this 'interference' might be put to best account. We have a saying—

Wedel England's difficulty is Ireland's opportunity.

Casement So I am here.

(Brief pause)

Wedel How was your crossing?

Casement Eventful. The British tried to intercept me twice. I had taken precautions, sent a power of letters from the ship written as though myself and my – manservant were a couple of women.

Wedel Really; what sort of things did you write?

Casement Oh, 'The dear kind Captain, such a nice man, a Dane with a beard just like cousin Roger's . . .' Or *(voice becoming for once effeminate:)* 'When the prize crew came aboard at Stornoway and I saw HMS *Hibernia* on their caps, I nearly kissed them . . .'

(Brief pause)

We slipped through their hands on that occasion. *(slight*

hint of paranoia:) The second attempt at interception came, when we berthed at Christiania, Norway – neutral territory. My – manservant, Adler, is himself a Norwegian; somehow or other he got himself kidnapped by British agents – on neutral territory – who hustled him off to their ambassador, Findlay. Who made an obscene proposal–

Findlay If you will deliver your master Casement to us, we will give you a thousand pounds.

Adler (*conventional Scandinavian accent*) No.

Findlay Two thousand pounds.

Adler No.

Findlay Come, come. Five thousand pounds. And personal immunity–

Adler I do not wish.

Findlay Free passage back to USA.

Casement But Adler's loyalty was a match for that. All the same, I could see the British would stop at no enormity to prevent me reaching here. I am convinced we were followed. When we left for the Baltic ferry, we went through Hell and high water to shake our shadows off: dodging in and out of store doorways; taking trams in one direction, then changing to trams moving in another; swopping taxis in midstream. I think altogether we are very clever to reach Berlin. I must protest, however, about your Customs Officers' treatment of Adler at Sassnitz: me they left alone, they roughed him up, his wallet was spilt, his fine gloves split down the seams.

Wedel They are only doing their job. Perhaps he frightened them, your fine son of Odin.

Casement Ay, he's a Viking right enough, and very – handsome. Even thon gap in his front teeth–

Wedel We have his picture.

Casement There was a Proosian on the train with us, eyed Adler all the way. He had a beard on him, projecting, stiff, divided in two sectors, one pointing right, one pointing left, and both were ugly.

Wedel What do you propose?

(*Brief pause*)

47

Count Bernstorff, Imperial Ambassador in New York, tells us you have a specific proposition to put to us. What is it?

Casement One, sir. To form an Extraordinary Legion from your Irish Catholic prisoners-of-war. Two: that your Imperial Government proclaim an intention – in return for such services as this Legion will provide – so far from annexing Ireland when you have won the war, as part of your victor's dispensation simply to sever Ireland from the British yoke.

Wedel What do you expect such a proclamation to achieve?

Casement A. An immediate setback to English recruitment in Ireland. B. A total commitment of Irish-American opinion to the Imperial German cause. Effecting, C – how shall I put it? – a beneficial veer in US foreign policy.

Wedel The moral effect, that Irishmen volunteer to fight against England, will be great. From our Intelligence in Ireland we learn that English recruitment is already low there. British propaganda resorts to crude lies, such as that Big Protestant Germany has violated gallant little Catholic Belgium and is raping her nuns.

Casement Belgian atrocities me arse: the lies of the British Press are colossal. Believe me, Sir: Imperial Germany not only shall win this war, she deserves to. By nature. I look at the manliness and brow of German bearing, their strong breasts turned fornenst a world of philistines and enemies. English newspaper trash about your 'barbarism' turns till spittle in my mouth. I regret I am not German.

German Announceress A hotel bedroom. Night. Casement's manservant the blond Norwegian, Adler, seated before the mirror of a splendid dressing-table, carefully making up his face.

Casement Adler, you are fearfully wasteful of money, we shan't have a pfennig left. You buy things you don't even need, more even than I do. Like this raincoat and gloves. I have no gloves, and you have six pairs.

German Announceress Adler goes on making up his face.

(*Cut in, loud: Codetta, First Movement Beethoven Op.* 57 *Sonata*)

A large aristocratic salon. An evening party. Count

48

Bluecher, aristocrat of the old style, talks with Casement, who is concealing his impatience with ill grace.

Bluecher ... Roger, this is not the London we were friends in. This is not Congo Reform. This is Berlin and war. Think carefully: what good ground beneath your feet here are you having really?

Casement I am in all the papers. Your editors would not biographize me so, if it did not suit your powers-that-be.

Bluecher Roger, with these 'powers' you have no real base. Listen what an old friend is adwizing, leave Germany before it is too late for you.

Casement Ireland matters, I do not.

Bluecher (*closer*) In London, people have the very dull eyes. Berliners are quick to see ... Your servant ...

Casement I will not hear a word against Adler. Not even from you. I owe him my life. Ambassador Findlay in Norway has already tried to estrange us, do not play their British game with me.

Bluecher ... Roger ... In the camp at Sennelager, Irish prisoners have been set apart. They are promised sport, a daily Mass, improved conditions. Two priests from Watican have arrived, a third from Philadelphia.

Casement Good.

Bluecher The Irish prisoners are complaining, to the Kommandant: rejecting such diwisive priwileges; asserting they are Irish Catholics *and British soldiers too.*

Casement Because they do not know their true allegiance. It is for that am I here.

German Announceress The prison camp. Snow is blowing. A wooden hut. NCOs of Irish regiments sit, squatted on the floor, under German guard. On a platform sit two German Brigadiers, between them stands Casement, thin white and tall, in overcoat with a rolled umbrella.

Casement A cáirde go lier—

(*Titters, ripple of bewilderment, amusement*)

Guards Schweig! Mundhalten!

An Irish NCO What?

A second (*mocks accent*) A cáirde go leir!

A third Spake King's English for Jazus' sake!

(Amused disturbance)

Guards Schweig! Schweig!

(Unquiet silence)

Casement I will be brief. Here are papers I have: the *Gaelic American*,
the *Continental Kerryman*—
First Irish NCO He's a Boo-er from Pretoria.
Third He's a bloody Fenian—
Casement At your leisure you are to peruse these—
A fourth *(mocks)* Per-yoose these—

(Amusement re-erupting:)

Casement I merely ask, which of yous Irish men will be willing to
fight, not for England, but for Ireland; under an Irish
flag; as honoured soldiers of the German government,
their special guests—!
Second Sure we're that already!

(Laughter)

Guards Schweig! Schweig! Mundhalten! Schweig!
Casement *(tries to ride disturbance)* Those that volunteer so can expect,
at the war's end if they so wish, free passage to America!
Second *(mocking)* Oh the 'land o' the free'!
Casement Those that do not must expect, through no fault of mine,
to be returned forthwith to the camps and conditions
from which they came–

(Silence)

German Announceress Wilhelmstrasse. An outer office. Casement and a clerk.
Casement No, I will not be content with Herr Meyer, he is a mere
errand-boy! Nor will I be content with von Wedel! I will
see the Chancellor, von Bethman-Hollweg! The Chancellor! At least von Jagow, Secretary of State – I insist on
the heads of government acknowledging I am here! I will
take their refusal as proof they do not entertain my
mission seriously.
Clerk Please. A message. For Herr Secretary, a message.
Casement Tell him this. I will not put two thousand Irish soldiers
into the treason pot without assurances on their behalf!
Tell him also, I see in this morning's London *Times* a list

of small nations a victorious Germany intends to liberate: where is Ireland? There is in this list no mention of Ireland—

Clerk I am sorry, Sir Roger, *The Times* must be mistaken—

Casement (*English thunder*) *The Times mistaken?!* – Oh, I know the game your Kaiser is playing. How can he commit himself to Ireland, ha? He still hopes for an accommodation with *London!* Tell Herr Secretary, the German mind-politic has all the insight of a pudding. Oh, where is that divine spark of insolence so quickens English piracy? I am sorry I have come.

German Announceress Hotel bedroom. Night. Casement lies in bed, unwell. Hears someone coming. Knows the step. His face lights up.

Casement Adler, you are safely back. How is Norway? What did you find out?

Adler Ambassador Findlay offered me ten thousand pounds this time. Just to bring you to his back door for the British to pick up—

Casement At least the British have the measure of me: they know my value. England is even sending an ambassador to the Vatican now: to pre-empt any influence of mine, the old Protestant cow will even reverse the Reformation!

Adler Findlay said you are a very clever son-of-a-bitch.

Casement (*gratified*) Aha.

Adler And added: But, he is a gentleman.

Casement I don't know I like that. Oh, what London wouldn't give to know exactly what I'm about!

English Announceress Keode rum at British Intelligence. German signals intercepted and dekoded.

German voices Wilhelmstrasse to Imperial German Embassy New York. Imperial Embassy New York to Sinn Féin HQ Dublin. Sinn Féin, from Berlin. Request more Irish priests as carriers. Re arms dispatch, propose land Shannon mouth. Casement payments, New York to arrange . . .

(*World War One bombardments:*)

German Crier O-yets! O-yets! Englant gebombt! Cities of Skarburg, Vitby and Vest Hartlipoolss visout mercy to smouldering ruinss gebombardiert!

Casement   Where are now the rats in their holes? And who will they
            think has put the Germans up to this, ha? I'll bet they're
            cursing their incompetence they ever let me through.

            (*Bombardments die down*)

            I'll tell you, Adler, what we'll do. We will singe England's
            beard. We will feed Ambassador Findlay with false
            reports: that I am . . . to be had for the taking, ha? On
            board a yacht. In the Skaggerak.
Adler   Whose yat?
Casement   Why, Norman Armour, the corned-beef king. The very
            man, his yacht is there. Now. What will England do?
            Findlay will alert them and they will send a squadron. The
            German navy will lie in wait, surround, and pounce.
Adler   I like Findlay.

            (*Pause*)

            I admire him, he's a man.
Casement   Why, what am I, then?
Adler   He stops at nothing, I admire that—
Casement   Where do I stop?
Adler   (*intimately close*) Scroddie. Scroddie. Take me to the
            prison camp.
Casement   I hardly think that would be wise. I don't know you
            would not be safer in Norway. Or better working for me
            in USA.
Adler   I want to come to your prison camp. Nice time . . .
Casement   That's just the trouble, honey child: you might fall for
            some Inniskilling Fusilier's cockade, and that would be
            calamitous.
Adler   I want to come wiv Scroddie to the pwison camp.
Casement   No!

            (*Silence*)

German Announceress   December twilight. Snow is falling. The wooden hut.

            (*Cahoots of laughter, uproar; barkings of German guards:*)

Guards   Still gestanden! Still stehen! Alle! Hier bleiben! Alle!
German Announceress   Casement is coming quickly out, protected by German

guards who are embarrassed. Others are running out after, with Casement's hat, coat, rolled umbrella.

(*Tumult of mockery from within*)

Now are two German Brigadiers from the hut outrunning, pursued by the Irish soldiers, who are hurling after them cardboard trays of little miniature Irish flags.

(*Tumult retreats*)

Casement The priests O Gorman and Crotty must do this job. They have more natural authority than I.

Brigadier The soldiers vill wolunteer, if ve give zem moneys.

Casement I have not the means. Nor would I consider that.

Brigadier Ve shall put more meat in their soup. Have ze Irish not ze national sonks they should be sinking?

Casement Ay, a harmonium might help. Ay: and maps of Ireland in their rooms!

Brigadier I think also, is good idea to have special uniform.

Casement Ye've something there. Ay. With golden harps. I see it. And shamrocks on the epaulettes!

Brigadier And ve should find too a special Cassolic commanding offitseer, of perfect English and many yokes.

Casement (*muttering*) But how shall I flush out that bastard Findlay? I know. Go to Norway myself . . . Ay: get von Wedel to provide me with a plain-clothes guard; go to Norway; get kidnapped – our bodyguards pounce on theirs and take them to the Norwegian neutral police! Force London's hand! A desperate idea . . . Pit my pennilessness, defencelessness, against all England's power and gold. Go out alone, to challenge in its dastardliness the mightiest government in the world . . . A desperate t'ing . . .

German Announceress But, Wilhelmstrasse. Von Wedel of the English Department looks up; sees, none too pleased, Casement ushered in, with the bloodshot eyes.

Wedel Yes? I thought you had gone to Norway.

Casement We took the wrong train. The British pre-empted me. The Baltic is a nest of submarines. I have a better idea.

Wedel Yes?

Casement An open letter.

Wedel What?

Casement An open letter! 'Dear Sir Edward Grey. Rub your Foreign Office nose in my faithful servant's Viking integrity when faced with the ignoble inducements of your Christiania tool—'

Wedel What are you talking about now?

Casement An open letter! To the American and European Press! I have a typer making twenty copies today: plus a special copy, specially bound, for the personal attention of the Pope himself! The English won't know where to hide themselves in the furore that will arouse! – You seem a little less than keen. The Austro-Hungarian ambassador is lunching with me tomorrow: he'll have it orchestrated sforzato in the Vienna Press. Show some intelligence.

German Announceress Berlin. Midmorning. A news kiosk. Casement buys eagerly of all foreign papers a copy: looks anxiously through each. Herr Meyer, Wilhelmstrasse staff, uneasily is joining him.

Meyer (*accent almost impeccable*) I fear they will not publish your letter in the Roman Press.

Casement Their new ambassador to the Vatican has seen to that.

Meyer And Lisbon were reluctant. But, see this.

Casement What does that say?

Meyer 'England prohibits all cables from the Continent.'

Casement To prevent my letter reaching America! – God in Heaven, how much more must this world endure from that Bitch and Harlot of the North Sea?! – Forgive me, Herr Meyer: even when one is fully well, and untroubled, it is not always easy to see things straight.

German Announceress A council in the German Chancellory. Present: Chancellor von Bethman-Hollweg; von Wedel, of English Department; von Jagow, Secretary of State. Chancellor von Bethman-Hollweg is looking puzzled at a postcard they have given him.

Chancellor (*slow*) Mistress . . . Shmit . . .

Wedel Smythe, Herr Chancellor.

Chancellor Mullin Ahr–

Wedel Mullingar, a town in Ireland, Herr Chancellor.

Chancellor Dear Mozzer . . .

Wedel This sentence, Herr Chancellor.

Chancellor 'Some lunatic . . . is trying to form an . . . Irish Legion . . . But we will die first.' (*pause*) This Kazement is a man of straw, yes? but can priests not succeed where he has failed?

Wedel The third, from Philadelphia, can not. The Irish prisoners resent his political abuse of the Confessional, and – boycott every Mass he gives.

Jagow Also, English and Scottish prisoners are pretending to be Irish, for the better food.

Chancellor (*carefully*) Is – chaos . . .

Jagow Herr Chancellor, such Irish Brigade as is already formed, is a drunken riff-raff, given to riot. The young commander we appointed for them has used up all his jokes. The Irish uniform designed by Casement is – womanly, with shamrocks and harps. Any soldier rash enough to put it on must endure catcalls and obscenities; and in the town meet jeering shouts 'Here comes an Englishman'.

Chancellor Is catastrophic. His valett, the Norvegian, we have spirited away: can not we get Kazement to America too?

Wedel If the English do not hang him first.

(*Marching sounds, ragged, few, shambolic:*)

[ain dhaw] *Casement* Aon dá, aon dá, aon, aon, aon dá . . . (*raises voice, tune-rhythm distorted to fit marchtime:*)
Oh I met wi Napper Tandy
ahn he tuik me by the hahn',
ahn I sayed 'How's dear oul Eyerlahn'
ahn how does she stahnd?'

(*Fade*)

Casement There, Herr Kommandant, our first route march done. We'll raise a force for Dark Rosaleen yet – Who is this?

Brigadier This is Captain Monteith. Irish Republican Army.

Monteith New York sent me.

Casement Oh how is Adler—?

Monteith (*ambiguous*) Cared for – You must realize there is no turning back from the road you have taken.

Casement How should there be? If it's right the road is.

Monteith Germany and England have agreed on an exchange of

	prisoners-of-war. London is interested in having only Irish prisoners from here. Why do you think that is?
German Announceress	February the tenth nineteen-sixteen. The German Chancellory.
Jagow	The matter of Casement's request, Herr Chancellor, that his Irish Brigade so-called be given weapon training. I find it utterly inappropriate. I find it dangerous. This rabble should not be given arms, leave alone be instructed in their use. How can we trust a man with such a history of changed allegiance? There was also, Herr Chancellor, his proposal we offer his 'brigade' for service with the Turks. I quote him: 'That will put Winston in his place, the bumptious ass'. Such a proposal affords an occasion of serious international indiscretion.
Chancellor	We are not compromised.
German Announceress	A message is brought in, for the Chancellor's eyes alone.

(Brief silence)

Chancellor	This Irish insurrection. It is timed for Easter Saturday. New York request arms dispatch to Lime Rick—
Jagow	Limerick—
Chancellor	To arrive Good Friday at the latest – What date is Good Friday?
Jagow	April twenty-first, Herr Chancellor.

(Brief pause)

Chancellor	Where is Kazement now?
Jagow	At a sanatorium in Munich, where he has nervous breakdown.
Chancellor	Is convenient. But even if the man were up and about, our assistance – if any – to this rebellion . . . is better negotiated with the Irish leaders in Dublin and America direct. There is no necessity for Kazement even to know this date. Doubtless he shall find it out in time. With luck, and his own erratic psychology on our side, he might then solve the problem of himself, himself.
English Announceress	Keode rum at British Intelligence. An intercepted message between German Foreign Office and New York Embassy.
German voices	SS Aud under Norwegian colours to land agreed arms

consignment: Tralee Bay April twenty-first. Signals as follows. All well, landing imminent: foxtrot india november november, finn, repeat, finn. Delay or abort: bravo romeo alfa november, bran, repeat, bran . . .

(Nineteen-sixteen railway station sounds)

German Announceress Night. Zoological Gardens Railway Terminal, Berlin. A waiting train, about to depart: destination plaque, 'Wilhelmshaven'. Three men: Casement, Monteith, a third, all dressed for long journey. An official of low rank, to see them away.

Casement . . . The Irish explosion seven hundred years a-coming, a fortnight away; and me, its chief possibilifier, the last told of it. Negotiations done over my head: two hundred thousand rifles at least we would have needed, a militia. What have they offered? Twenty thousand Russian rifles, out of date . . . The volunteering done behind my back: how many? One. One, one, a Daniel Bailey: and how do I know it's not only a ploy on his part to escape? . . . The Rising is suicide. It must be stopped.

(Whistle-blast. Soon train is starting up)

So whither now does my road go? What Casement is this that travels it? A coward, or a fool? I do not know. But go I must . . .

Official Sir Roger! Sir Roger! You are forgetting! You will need this! Your sleeping-ticket!

(Train louder, gathers speed. Cut)

X

(Inside aircraft. Priest-drone fades down. Intercom switches on)

Irish air hostess Ladies and gentlemen. In a few moments we shall be landing at Baldonnel Airfield, County Dublin. Please fasten your safety belts and extinguish all cigarettes. You are requested not to move from your seats until after the aircraft has completely stopped. Thank you. Támid

anbuich dibh go rinne sibh an turas seo linn inniu. Slán
agus beannacht libh.

Casement (*voice acquiring a dark regionless formalized Irishness*) To land
in Ireland. Step on Irish ground . . . Feel again the touch
of her in heel and sole . . . That moment of landing, that
moment, all a whole system in me, current with especial
love, grief, joy, pain, runs live again; that old self,
slumbering, forgot, each time I come again to step on
Irish ground, with pride and tears awakes again . . . Such
tears . . . Such the Poles weep who carry native earth
with them around the world . . . That moment, stepping
down from gangplank ontil Irish soil, that quickening.
To land on Ireland, put my foot on Irish ground . . .

(*Soft breakersounds fade up*)

Good Friday morning, dark small hours, April twenty-
first, nineteen-sixteen. Drag myself up through the
breakers, to the dry of the Atlantic Kerry shore. Weak.
Sick. After twelve days and nights in a U-boat cabin
unable to sleep, scarce able to breathe. And now, no sign
of any light or signal from the land, to welcome us;
expecting us. None.

Our dinghy overturns. Again. I can hardly haul my
weight ashore. I lie at the waterline an hour, unable to
move.

It grows light. We bury our pistols, binoculars, rifle-
stocks; hide the dinghy in the dunes. We stop at a stream,
wash the mud and the brine from our clothes, wring them
as dry and clean we can. Primroses, wild violets all
around; skylarks soaring in the air: I am in Ireland,
for all my sickness and dread the happiest I have been for
a year and more. God's Will I am here.

But nobody to welcome us. Nobody has expected us to
come.

A man comes, driving a cart of seaweed in the dawn. We
hide, in an old earth fort. Bailey and Monteith go off, to
find the local Volunteers and bring a car. I wait in the
rath alone. The day grows warm.

Twenty past one: a policeman finds me. I pretend, for the
last time in my life, to be an Englishman. An autha, an

English autha, eout for a streoll – He sees my clothes stiff with mud and brine. I see him see. I see my death is real, fixed, near. A boy with a ponytrap comes by. The police commandeer him. I try to tear up a German cipher-message in my hands behind my back.

Tralee. The town's air mutinous, in that peculiar smouldering Irish way. I wait by the turffire in the Constabulary billiard room: for Monteith, the Volunteers to spring me. None come. A doctor. I whisper to him who I am. The door is open, guard light: it will be easy. He goes. A priest. I whisper to him the Rising must be stopped. I am a priest, he says, not a go-between. But he goes. No one comes.

Saturday morning. I am marched to the train through the streets of Tralee. Many must have watched, from behind curtains and out, and known me going to my death. No finger lifted. The train leaves. Killarney. Mallow. We change. Dublin. Military Barracks, Arbour Hill. Stripped and searched. Marched, dropping with sleep, to the boat train: *SS Ulster*, for Holyhead. The steward kind. 'God bless you, Sir.' He brings me cigarettes.

Sunday six a.m. Euston. Escorted to the Yard by Inspector Sandercock of CID. A proper and courteous man, I wish him well. There are such Englishmen.

Interrogation. Heads of Naval Intelligence, CID; two or three others. A shorthand-writer. Who am I? I tell them. There may be many people masquerading with that name just now, they say. I doubt, I say, if many will wish to. Shorthand-writer sent from the room. As he goes, he murmurs: Greater love hath no man. I will name no names. They say, if I do, it will remove some innocent from suspicion. I am not trapped. At last they say the charge will very likely be High Treason. I hope so, I say: you have failed to win the hearts of Ireland while you still had one chance left.

To the Tower. Incommunicado eleven days, unshaven, in clothes still damp and briny from the sea. Cell infested with lice: after a few hours my head, neck, arms a tissue of bites. Three men on death-watch, eyes never off me night or day, the light on all the time, no shade: no sleep possible, every thought a page of Hell. I expected cousin Gertie at least to visit me.

Gertrude (*strong, gentle, plain; rather Quaker in tone*) I tried. Home Secretary refused to see me: such an interview could be granted only by the Secretary for War. Secretary for War refused to see me: Home Office I must ask. I said Home Office sent me here. So then they said, The Yard are involved, ask there. No reply. I wrote to the Governor of the Tower, begging him at least to tell Roger I was trying to see him. Refused. I walked round the Tower, trying to make my thoughts of Roger penetrate through those walls to him. A solicitor was found at last to take the case. He had to resign his partnership for doing so. He asked permission to visit Roger to discuss the defence. Refused. He wrote to Asquith. Refused. Home Office again. Sent on to Secretary for War again. This time, 'Treasury involved, go there'. The man at the Treasury: 'I have no influence; a military matter; best thing to do is nothing.' I said: 'If it's a military matter, why are the Yard so interested, and the Treasury?' The man turned cruel, vicious, snarled at me. As a last resort we went to the Regiment at the Tower. A Major showed some courtesy: he promised to intervene. Permission given. Roger thought he was going to be shot: that was why we had come, to say goodbye. I told him how we had tried. He said 'Damn these people who tell me lies and try to break my heart'. One guard had disobeyed orders, spoken to him: 'We're all very sorry for you, Sir; we think you're a brave man and hope you'll get off.' That soldier was never on guard again. A lady Roger had known then wrote to Asquith a description and complaint of Roger's treatment in the Tower: she threatened to send a copy to America.

Casement I was moved to Brixton. A hospital diet; powders to ease the itching on my arms and head. I planned to conduct my own defence, Shaw drafted me one. Then I thought, Attorney-General now is Frederick Edwin Smith, old third in that Ulster Covenant with Carson and Craig. A political score to settle, he'll bar no holds in annihilating me.

Despair. What course? but make one last great speech; turn; go. At other times a consuming will to survive: I would work like a madman on my brief.

I could not decide my best defence. I could hardly think clear. I was tormented thinking, how easily I might have succeeded, had only one act of mine somewhere turned out, however slightly, better than it did. My counsel, Sullivan, an Irishman, last of the old rank Serjeant-at-Law, was alien to English practice, kept on saying he hoped the worry would not kill him. He argued my moral allegiance to Ireland was no defence in law. He sought to acquit me on a technicality.

Sullivan   The Statute under which you are indicted is a Treason Act of thirteen-fifty-one in ancient language, and capable of interpretation in two opposing ways. The Statute's defining clause is so punctuated – or rather, so *un*-punctuated – as to seem to apply to offences done at home and abroad. But, if I insert a comma here, so, so far from merely separating offences done abroad, one could construe it as – *excluding* them. The question is, was such a comma ever there? We have reason to believe there was.

Casement   In the midst of a war? try to persuade an English jury to acquit an Irish 'traitor' on the strength of a medieval comma that may or may never have been there? As well refer the keeping of Lent to a jury of butchers.

Preliminary trial. How white my hand has suddenly become, blue veins on it standing out like string. A woman's hand . . . I fidget, scratch my neck, bite my nail, pinch my cheeks, squeeze my eyes; look up at the ceiling, down at the floor; reach into my breast pocket, pull out nothing; raise my eyebrows, relax them, deepen the furrows on my head. A shadow, the man of me gone.

Evidence from exchangee Irish prisoners-of-war. My speeches, gestures at the Limburg camp thrown back at me: mine, undeniable; mine, unrecognizable. What Casement these prisoners depict! poor, ridiculous, a scarecrow. Their voices I loved, a cadence, a turn of phrase – such memories . . . And I was full of grief for them. Some accents so thick, Bench and witness can hardly understand each other. 'How eold is your daughtah?' 'A hundhred yaards.' The trial date is fixed.

Gertrude   Oh Roger, why did you do it? I said. He said, To drag Ireland up on to the stage of the world; get her to look ahead. Don't look at my boots, he said: they're in an awful state since I landed; and my laces they've taken away. He dreaded his trial, he said; regretted he had lived so long, to have this ordeal as his last end.

Casement   Monday June twenty-six. My trial begins. A new dock built, for the jury all to see me clear. The language of the indictment new-modernized, I its first offering. Dressed my best, suit tight like a glove: cuff-kerchief, tie-collar, westcot-shirt, a study in white-and-black. Court full; an atmosphere, the papers said, of that serene impartiality makes British Justice a wonder of the world. On the Bench one judge, Horridge, Porridge, some such name, had a facial twitch, made him look like a death's-head under a wig.
Attorney-General's opening address: no overt partisanship, all polemic and invective subtle and implied. He spoke of my 'considerable career of public usefulness', my pension – though I'd ceased to draw that when I went to America – and made great play of my 'fulsome' knighthood letter to the King. What baneful conversion, he asked, had I suffered since then, for me, when England my benefactress fell from Imperial opulence to struggle for survival in a bitter war, me then to desert her? He described my time in Germany: myself in a mirror again; but not the man shown there. The facts might be in this indictment; the truth was not.

Gertrude   I was told the prisoner was traditionally allowed one visitor at lunch. The warder said I must ask the Lord Chief Justice's permission for this. *He* said Home Office. I took a taxi there, sent in a letter of request. Home Secretary gave me leave, sent me back with a covering note to the Court. As I gave this in and saw it open in the Judge's hand, I saw it was *my* note, endorsed in red: Request to be granted by no means.

Casement   The second day. The Kerry witnesses. A farmer, saw us landing as he came home in the small hours from a holy well. A servant-girl, as usual up at four, had seen the three of us go by beyond a wall. Then evidence of the arms-ship's scuppering, her cargo of rifles of Russian make, nineteen-o-five. It was part of the Prosecution's case that England was at war: the law required this proving formally. The Declaration itself was displayed in court as evidence. The Prosecution closed.

Gertrude Remembering how we had been deceived the day before, I asked the warders if at least I could send Roger in some lunch. One said Surely, the other No. Home Secretary. Home Office again. The Legal Adviser there, Sir Ernley Blackwell. Pale, narrowfaced, lips thin: a man of ice, ranking charity love and joy in their proper legal place, among the futilities of life. 'I have come, Sir Ernley, to ask permission to send some lunch in to Sir Roger Casement at the Courts.'

Blackwell (*the actor should play up whatever grain of gentleness he can find*) That is impossible.

Gertrude You mean you forbid it.

Blackwell I have no power to allow it.

Gertrude The Court Officials assure me that you have.

Blackwell I fear I cannot do it.

Gertrude You mean you will not.

(*Brief pause*)

I beg you, be humane enough.

Blackwell I have no power.

Gertrude You have—

Blackwell I regret I cannot continue this interview.

Gertrude I regret I cannot leave. Until you grant me my request.

(*Brief pause*)

Blackwell If I do, it must be understood that this is the only matter in which a concession can be made.

Gertrude I accept that. Will you please telephone the Courts now, to confirm that you have permitted this?

Blackwell It is enough for you to tell them I have done so.

Gertrude I would prefer that you telephoned now; or else gave me a note.

Blackwell I will give you no note.

Gertrude I cannot leave.

(*Pause*)

Blackwell I will telephone.

Casement Defence. The medieval comma: through two hot afternoon hours, Sullivan and Bench floundered in a morass of
archaism and technicality. His contention disallowed.

Next morning, a brief speech from me, rebutting in my
most English voice certain innuendoes I felt endangering
me. I had never arranged for those Irish prisoners' food
to be reduced who did not join my Brigade. I had never
advised Irish prisoners to fight with the Turks – a
prevarication: I had suggested something such. I had
never asked an Irishman to fight for Germany. Most
important, and absolute: I never took one penny of
German gold.

Sullivan embarked on his climactic argument in my
defence. Treason, he said, is to be judged by intention,
not by deed. He sought to identify all my acts with my
commitment to Ireland, Ireland alone, whoever my
helpers happen to be. He alluded to the Attorney-General:
had not he himself, with Carson and Craig, bought
German assistance against the King? This part of
Sullivan's speech I thought the best; the rest was
casuistry and full of holes. But he did his best for me. He
had not slept three days nor nights for worry; all the red
in his blood was drained. So now, when he was rebuked
for mentioning the Carsonites, he was ordered to apologize for bad practice. Bench then said he had listened with
increasing impatience to the diminishing relevance of
this speech. Sullivan's thread was snapped. He fumbled,
fell silent; collapsed. I watched them help him away. It
seemed the logical poetic thing to happen at this climax
of the trial for my life.

Thursday. The public gather for the kill. My defence
continued by a subordinate reading from Sullivan's notes.
He was inexperienced, hampered by constant cautions
and rebukes. Yet I liked his speech better. His contentions
had more substance. He argued that the allegations
pertained more properly to the Defence of the Realm Act,

and did not legally qualify for a charge of High Treason. He rightly abjured all plea for special sympathy for me. I thought him very good.

Attorney-General summarized. My various pleas he dismantled one by one. My claim I had sought only to arm the South against Carson, he mocked as a post factum invention, an 'exhumed defence' from the accusing biography in which I now found myself. Had not the war made nonsense of such controversies? My arguments of intention, allegiance, he flayed; left stripped to the bone my actual consortment with an actual enemy. Not my mind nor my heart must the jury judge, but what I had done, at the time that I had done it.

In the lunchbreak I put final touches to my speech from the dock.

Court resumes. Lord Chief Justice directs the jury scrupulously but leaves them no alternative: if an Irish Rising weakens an England at war, then assisting England's enemy I am. Two fifty-three, the jury retire. Twelve minutes to four, they are back. I see on their faces what their verdict is.

Now my great moment, the Irishman's traditional great moment: the speech from the dock, my last appearance in the living world. I had worked on that speech for weeks: few writers ever have a job like that. I spoke for half an hour. I disdained the jurisdiction of the Court; the moral irrelevance of a medieval law enacted by an Edward, King of England King of France, who now today could strain no strand round any Frenchman's neck, yet whose dead hand today could stretch out over centuries to throttle an Irish man whose sovereign he never was: that phantom the King, can *that* still be dug up from the dungeons of an age of darkness, to tear life and limb from a man for choosing which is his allegiance more, to his oppressor against an outer enemy, or to the folk of his own land? I put my eye on F. E. Smith before me, speaking of those who for party and gain misuse the ardour and passion of the Irish North, whose interest in Ireland lies only in her degradation and division, to serve their clubroom animosities. Some choose, I said, through Irish politics a path might lead to the Woolsack; I, a road must lead to the Dock. Here today such a two of us stand, and I'll not change places with that other man for all the world.

Smith murmured aloud: 'Nor I with him, no fear', or some such words; put his hands in his pockets; and lounged from the Court.

Hot now. The tension sundered. Restlessness. It was the sentence the public were waiting to hear, nothing else. I saw my peroration must be brief. For what then, I said, may the Irishman die? For Flanders? Yes. For Belgium? Yes. For a patch of Mesopotamian sand? a rocky trench on the heights of Gallipoli? Why, so he might. Thus, we are told, we are winning self-government for Ireland. And when we are so dead, will that promise be honoured? May they fight for Ireland? No. For then they are traitors, their deaths and their dreams dishonourable alike. Ireland, that has wronged no man, injured no land, sought no dominion over any, now is treated like a convict among the nations of the earth. If it be 'treason' to fight an unnatural condition such as that, then 'traitor' let me ever be.

The judges put on their black caps, tiredly, clumsy, askew. Sentence given. To be hanged. I bowed to the Bench. I smiled.

Pentonville. The cell for the condemned. Dress, a blue convict-suit with arrows, a felon's cap. Prisoner one two seven o. The Governor nagged me every day with diatribes against my treachery: why had Ireland not waited until England was free? Not cricket, I suppose.

An appeal, of course. Petitioners like Drinkwater, Arnold Bennett, C. P. Scott, GBS, Galsworthy, Conan Doyle. Arthur said my tropical investigations had put me to serious strain: bless him. But he had contributed seven hundred pounds to my defence. GBS wrote I had no standing in Ireland at all, the trial gave me that; I was still no hero there, the hangman would make me that. Appeal on two counts: that damnable comma; and a contention that, in identifying the Rising – in which I had played no part – with aiding an enemy, Lord Chief

Justice had misdirected. I know now two members of that jury would have dissented from the verdict, had they heard my speech before. For some reason I never discovered, the plea of misdirection was never lodged. The appeal concerned itself with that comma alone. Dismissed: I am the King's liege wherever I may be. Clear enough. My hanging fixed. For August the third.

I digest the reality of my own approaching death. I feel the need to identify with the Irish nation through their predominant faith. My mother, a Catholic, forced by my father to renounce, had secretly baptized me as a child. But now I needed to be rationally convinced. Fathers visited me. But one said the Westminster Cardinal wished me first to repudiate my scandalous public and private acts. I could not. All I had done, was of my self. But in the end, I was received.

Gertrude I lost the teaching post I had held without reproach for seventeen years. I went to see Roger one last time. The Governor had been nagging him again. Roger said, 'What will you do when it is all over?' I said, Don't, don't, I can't think of that. He said, 'Go back to Ireland. Take my body with you. Don't let me lie here in this dreadful place. Take my body and bury it in Antrim, in the old church yard at Murlough Bay.' I said, I will. I wept. It was the only time I was ever with him I wept. He said, he said – 'I don't want to die and leave all you dear ones, but I must.' I said, It won't happen: there are petitions, we shall prevent it. He said, 'Don't cod yourself. They want my death . . .' The warders marched him out. He turned at the door and said Goodbye, God bless—

(Brief pause)

I went. In the corridor I wept out loud, I couldn't help it. A warder said Go. He said, You must go. He took me across the prison yard to a warder with keys. I was crying all the time. The warder with keys was opening the gate – Stop, I said, I can't go yet. I could hardly stand, my sobs were shaking me. Go, he said. You must go. 'Get a policeman to get me a taxi', I said, 'I can't go out in the street like this.' Pull yourself together, he said. Now go.

Casement I watched the last sunset of my life. I stood in the yard, and watched the sun sink down beyond the prison wall. My last day, finished. I came back into my cell. I asked for paper, and wrote my last thoughts down. England has no claim on Ireland, in Law, Morality nor Right. I die in the Catholic faith, I accept it fully now. Bury me in Ireland. If I shed tears at the gallows in the morning they will be nature's tribute wrung from sorrow, not from cowardice. The brave are not ashamed to weep. Strange ... Strange ... I feel as though they were going to kill in me a boy, my hands so free of blood. I do not comprehend how anyone should want to hang me. Who are the traitors? Lift up your hearts. All are my brothers now.
I slept. I had been sleeping better. All was good now. I knew that all was good now.
When I awoke, the sun was up before me. 'A glorious day!' I said. They dressed me in my ordinary clothes. The fathers said a Mass. I made my First Communion. I took breakfast. Then I prayed. The prison doctor asked me, was there anything he could do? Nothing. Nine struck. The Governor came, the Sherriff, Ellis the executioner, his assistant. My hands were pinioned behind my back. The clergy before, we moved in procession to the execution shed, next door. I listened to the Litany for the Dying, I made the responses obediently. I saw the noose. The lever. The trap. For me. I stepped on to the trap. I saw that I was taller than them all. Ellis strapped my ankles together. He threaded the noose below my jaw. I said, Lord Jesus receive my soul. I heard the lever pull

(*Silence*)

XI

(*Rainsqualls. Whine of aircraft approaching, landing, taxi-ing to halt:*)

Irish Announceress (*voice not so soggy as air hostess'*) Baldonnel Airfield, county

Dublin. Tuesday the twenty-third of February nineteen-sixty-five. Dark evening, cold, the runway swept with squalls of sleet. The aircraft bringing home to Ireland the symbolic remains of Roger Casement touches to earth; runs, slows, halts; stands. Dignitaries of the Irish State; high-ranking Army officers; an escort of Captains one hundred strong: gather solemnly to welcome him.

(*Aircraft engines off*)

A chosen Captain goes aboard. He drapes the coffin with the Irish flag. The coffin is brought slowly out. The escort present arms; reverse arms.

(*Muted sounds of this*)

The coffin of Casement is borne, in solemn march, to lying-in-state.

(*Opening of Mahler V – Funeral March, scored for Military Winds, Percussion: unblended, eldritch, hard. Fade down at String Melody (Bar 35 seq.) (i.e. it must sound like a Band, not a Symphony Orchestra, on this airfield). Slowmarch footfalls.*)

Casement (*hollow*) And I am dead. I have no eyes. I have no touch, to feel this land beneath my feet; I have no tread. Help me, help me—

Captain (*young, gentle*) Sir?

Casement Who are you?

Captain The chosen Captain, Sir.

Casement Tell me where I am. What is this street? Where am I being taken now?

Captain First, Sir, to the Garrison Church of Saint Loreto and Saint Brigid, to consecrate your return. Then to a lying-in-state at the Church of the Sacred Heart at Arbour Hill.

Casement Arbour Hill. Arbour Hill, where I was stripped and searched after my arrest, it has black memories for me—

Captain Black memories for all Ireland, Sir. Here was the trench of lime where the bodies of the Easter Patriots were thrown.

(*Cut*)
(*Dim creakings, obscure in silence of Empty Church*)

Irish Announceress	Church of the Sacred Heart, at Arbour Hill. Dark. The coffin lies in state. Casement at night, receives strange visitors.
Elderly Anglo-Irishman	Colonel Arthur Lynch, Boer Army. In MacBride's illegal Irish Brigade I fought against the British for six months. I too was tried: Carson my prosecutor. I too was sentenced to death. My sentence commuted. A few weeks in prison, then released. Then pardoned. I ended my days as a Westminster MP. What grace had I, that you had not?
Young Kerryman	John MacCarthy, farmer, Curraghane, Kerry. On my road home through the dark that morning, after praying at a holy well – I said – saw your boat and the dagger in it; then sent for the RIC. I am sorry.
Young Kerry girl	Mary Gorman, farmgirl, saw yous that morning pass the gate. They said to me What time was that? Half-four, I said. Four thirty? they said. I said, My usual hour to be up is four. – I'm sorry.
Elderly Kerryman	Michael Hussey, him in the daybreak was driving seaweed in a cart. Yous thought yous three had hid from me. In the rath. But I was after seeing a strange light flash at sea the night before. I'm sorry.
Young Kerry boy	Martin Collins, with the pony and trap. At the rath. I seen ye tear a paper up in your hands behind ye, and went back later to see what it was. It was a code, I took it to the polis. I'm sorry what I done.
Middle-aged Kerryman	(*professional class accent*) Doctor Shanahan, the doctor you spoke to in the Barracks at Tralee. I went to get what help I could. But all were under strict orders to do nothing that might abort the Insurrection. I am sorry.
Youngish Kerry priest	Father Ryan, the priest you spoke with in the Barracks at Tralee. You whispered in my ear the Rising must be stopped. I got your message through. A countermand, in any case, went out: and half the Rising got it, half did not, so it was all postponed a day, so then the regions did not rise. Dublin alone was easy for the Britishers to quench.
Middle-aged Irish-American	John Devoy, leader of the Irish in America. Oh Casement, Casement, impractical guy, we never dreamed the ruin you would do. Those rifles had been good enough for Russia to overrun East Prussia with, our fellows could

have shot a good few Englishmen with those – if once they'd only got their hands on them. Casement, you say your sex was your patriotism's seed. I say, Wasn't it your undoing too? Your angel Adler we had to hold in America by force, he was all for going to London to testify against you. He was in the pay of the English all along.

Sullivan Sullivan. Time and time again over, I might perhaps have saved your life. The English were determined to get you hanged, their brains sore put to it to devise the correctest means of trying you first. Then they smelled the odium that was earning them in the world, and reached for any straw, to stop your death-machine. But *my* one hope was to show the Treason Act did not apply. I could have appealed on the misdirection. Perhaps I should have done. It would have failed. Perhaps I should have done ... My appeal was all over the head of that comma. Justice Aitken and Justice Darling–

Aitken We looked at the original of the Statute at the Records Office–

Darling We pored over it for hours–

Aitken We even used a magnifying glass–

Darling No comma–

Aitken No punctuation break–

Darling Of any kind.

Aitken Nothing.

Darling, Aitken We are sorry.

Sullivan Objective examination I still believe will show the Treason Act does not apply. Even if it did, it did not have to. You were a sacrifice. For Easter Week, nothing you actually did, were you to be hanged. I made the right decisions ... Such hard decisions ... I could have saved your life ... But at what cost ... Your reputation ... Such hard decisions ...

Asquith I, Asquith, Prime Minister, called Cabinet three times to see if any legal loophole could be found. Reprieve pure and simple would have shown weakness, and possibly brought the government down. Insanity could not be established: your bearing and intellectual command in Court showed that. But then came into our hands a copy

71

of your treaty with the Germans, to use the Irish Legion against us in the Middle East. There could be no talk of mercy after that. So Blackwell said—

Blackwell Let the law take its course. Then put the diaries to judicious use, to prevent the man attaining martyrdom.

Asquith A sorry business.

Cockney Warder I'm the warder that whistled while you was makin up your dyin speech. I umbly apologize. No, onest. But put yourself in my shoes, mate, the bloody bawdom: all my life spent tahelling bleedin prisoners dahn.

Casement (*weak*) Ay, towelling prisoners down, there goes the history of it all. Warders and prisoners in that great prison England; Empire; that prison, the world. And where is the far-seeing brain that governs all? Dwells by some Westminister* fountainhead, in linen fine . . .

(*Amorphous hushed shuffle of large crowd in echoing uneasy Cathedral silence*)

Irish Announceress The Catholic proCathedral, Dublin.
The coffin of Casement lies in public state.

Child Why is it a proCathedral, Mammy? Why isn't it a Cathedral, why is it a *pro*Cathedral, Mammy?

Mammy Till we get the two Cathedrals back they took from us. Make way for the nuns, dear.

Nun . . . He was an Irishman—

Second Nun A true Irishman.

Third Nun He died for Ireland. A wonderful Catholic end, thanks be to God.

First Nun A Catholic death.

Third Nun Noble.

Second Nun True Irishman, he was . . .

A Student from Trinity College Dublin I cannot and do not believe a sodomite lies there.

Second TCD Student What does it matter now?

First TCD Student The case for a total forgery is very persuasively argued in an article in *Threshold* . . .

Boy What's in the box, Ma?

Ma Coffin.

Boy What's in the box, Ma?

* *Pronounce as spelt.*

72

Ma A hero of Ireland. A martyr.

Boy Is it a man, Ma? Is it a man?

A philoprogenitive Irish mother (*calls, rebukes, variously hisses to her brood near and far*) Felim. Eu-gene! Felim, Seán! *Seán!* Teresa. Dominic. Seán, Seán! Fionula, Eumon – Brigid! Here Vincent and Patrick, give over – Dymphna! Colum, Eunan, Patrick—!

Third Nun And every fifth one blessed by a bishop.

Progenitive mother Make way for the Father. Joseph, make way for the Father! Eu-gene! Let the priest in the queue, Eugene!

A Professional Irishwoman Sure what does it matter what the fella did? Hasn't he the right? The great Gaels of Ireland are the men that God made mad. Chesterton wrote that. And he was an Englishman to boot.

(*Long long upcurving electronic anthropoid cry, breaking at last at peak into a frisson-percussion collapse like opening of vast pores, cold:*)

Irish Announceress The proCathedral, night: the coffin on the catafalque, haunted by the ghosts of Ireland in the moments of their death.

(*Sounds modulate to high slow-throbbing whine, suggesting pain:*)

A Dano-Irish soldier Soldier, from the battle of Clontarf. My skull is being split. Half Dane, half Irelander. King Brian Boroimhe when I am dead, will lash my body upright to an* post like all his other dead. Then the Danes will think our Irish numbers are not growing less. My skull, split skull, one little penny in Ireland's freedom's price. Mac Aulay, son of Olaf, is my name . . .

A Norman-Irish lord By order of King Henry Tudor my neck is thrawn, my privities are removed; my stomach is slit, my entrails gathered out, a screaming knot – This filthy ˙pain, a Tyburn holiday, reward for rebellion. Now for your écarteling, Irish, Norman, FitzGerald of Kildare . . .

A screaming child Child of Wexford, rolled down Enniscorthy Hill in a Cromwell barrel spiked inside with nails!—

Belfast man (*accent anachronistic*) Wolfe Tone: now says, Orange ahnd green, stahnd free of yuir retarding myths; see whui yuir anamy is! Stand up! Be sons no more. Be brothers. – Now the knife. Stretch throat. Blade to flesh. Incise —

* *Pronounce as spelt.*

Wexford youth Pike lad of Leinster, ninety-eight. I spoke a brand of Flemish with my granda till the day he died. At moonrise I upped with a pike like the others and followed a brave priest. Now the English have me, and a pitchcap on my head. Here is a soldier with a torch, to make candles of us all.

O Connell Daniel O Connell, king without a crown, die in disgrace. Alone of all your heroes, Gael of the Gaels. Machinery of repression can be used against itself; but only so far. Believe, if you like, you can win within the system: I say this, it is a debilitating trick. The system-men have always a higher trump to play than any they will condescend to let you hold.

Fenian A Fenian, hanged the day Casement you were three years old. One message I have, one message only. Violence, they tell you, is an answer to nothing. Yet it is always the answer *they* first give. What just reform was ever peacefully begun?

Parnell Parnell. Squire, Protestant, half American; King of Ireland never crowned. Ireland, Ireland, thralling harlot, witchery you have; we love you for your beauty, face of a hag, mouth the arsehole of a pig. I've feet of clay: your panders pounced; you've never forgiven me, nor forgiven yourselves for not forgiving me. Casement, Casement, Franco-Manx ex-Presbyterian Ulster sodomite, my clay was only ankle-high, you're filth to the belt: what talisman of Irishness for God's sake will this bitch accept? Or is she already too much bought, and too much sold? Women of Ireland, look to your rank: high in mystery, and lower than the cow.

Pearse Pearse, Plunkett, MacDonagh, MacDiarmada, Ceannt, Connolly, Clarke, Colbert, Daly, O Hanrahan, Mallin, Heuston, Pearse, MacBride. Shot at Easter, laid in lime. And even I, Patrick Pearse, part English. Casement, where are you in these? What symbol are *you*, in this dance of death? What is *your* relevance?

(Coda of Liszt Csárdás Macabre on metallous piano-strings – abnormally deep, slow-stretched, echoing, black, electronically deformed. Also, muffled drumbeats, funereal:)

Casement My relevance is, that I am coming Home. We are moving northwards. Oh, if I could see, if I could only feel the air . . . Captain, what day is it?

Captain A Monday, Sir, the first of March.

Casement What weather is in it?

Captain Cold, Sir. It will snow.

Casement I'm going north now, amn't I?

Captain This street leads north.

Casement How far am I from home?

Captain Not far.

Casement What street is this?

Captain O Connell. It was called Sackville in your time.

Casement Why then we're in Dublin yet. We've a ways to go. Up country to the Boyne, Cromwell's Drogheda; through the Gap o' the North where the Brown Bull fought the White, and died in his own hills. Down between the halves of Newry; up past Slieve Gullion to Armagh. Then out till Antrim and the sea . . . Amn't A right?

(Silence. Vague Requiem-sounds dimly filter:)

Why are we stopped? Whose funeral is this, blocking our road?

Captain (uneasy) Yours, Sir.

Casement (at last) We done the journey quick.

Captain This is Glasnevin.

Casement (at last) Oh ay. But not to bury me. Not here. To do some liturgical thing for my return, but not to bury me, not here—

Captain The plot is chosen, Sir, your sister marked it out—

Casement God bless her dear heart; but it's against my wish – It—

Captain Hush, Sir, hush, please—

Casement (speech gradually becoming stage Ulster again) I'll not lie in a Dublin 'll do this to me – An Ireland 'll disregard me so, it is another lie – Not such an Ireland, *I will not lie here*—

Captain Whisht Casement, the President is making a moving speech, your biographers have come, there's not a dry eye in the graveyard—

Casement (choked fury) Not here, not here, I will not lie here—

Captain Quit thrawin' in your coffin man, for God's sake, the Cardinal himself is lookin' our way – Keep still in there, lie still – His Eminence is comin' over, oh my God—

The Cardinal (*Dublin gutter speech*) Hey. Lie back down in there!

Casement Eminence my arse—

Cardinal Casement, lie down!

Casement Why not in Antrim, then? Cardinal? What trick is this?

Teeshakh President, Taoiseach, what lie is this? Why not in Antrim, to my specific dying wish?

Cardinal Balls to your specific dying wish, we've got you now.

Casement Am I a property, then? Eminence? A relic of sacred bones? Oh, don't let your young men in their worship come too near till *me*! And my writings, will *they* be a national treasure, too? Or will they go down on your index, Tubberguts DD?

Cardinal I'm disgusted at you. Lie down. Be a good hero, shut your mouth. Be a good patriot, lie down.

Casement (*quite Paisley-like*) I'll not lie here! Sand me till Pantonville again! Next time, do the job right! Straight! Oh Ireland, weeper of tears for a man yous do not know nor want to know, I'll not lie here, give me the huppucruts of England, at least I am an honest anamy there! (*climax*) I'd liefer be a traitor by their lights than a patriot by these!

Cardinal Down with him. Get him under. Quickly. Quickly!— Down!

Casement Not here! (*voice suddenly lost beyond*) Not here . . .!

(*Brief silence. Fade up deep moaning of cold wind, comfortless, reminding of the Wind of Time (VII): no Gothick. Sustain throughout:*)

. . . Cold grave, cold . . . Alone . . . In cold grave, cold, and far from home . . .

Irish Announceress Night. Glasnevin. The funeral is gone. The cemetery is empty: but for one figure, by the new-filled grave. A youth. He is bleeding, and maimed from an explosion. Slow snow is falling.

Youth (*speech formalized Ulster, gentle; a voice completely new to us. A hint that he is shock-shattered to the limit of endurance*) No, Casement; you are not your lone.

Casement A Northern voice. Whose voice is that?

Youth A patriot, not yet born. I cannot see my road. Tell me my road.

Casement Dagh, how should I know?

Youth Because you're dead.

Casement Ay. I am dead.

Youth Snow's falling on your grave. Do ye not feel it? First snow after a funeral makes the buried doubly dead.

Casement Why am I here? Buried for ever, far from home . . .

Youth We'll have to dig ye up again.

Casement Why this – bungle?

Youth Carson and them ones won. The Black Pig Dyke of ancient days has been revived. There is a Border. Where you'ld lie is on that other side. Our side.

Casement Now I understand. The job's not done. Relevance on relevance, me in my life a symbol of Ireland's seceding, a token of her fracture in my death: an exile even in my grave. Am I to have no rest from paradoxical significance? Have I to be exhumed and buried yet again?

Youth They say but for the Border Hitler might well have won the Atlantic War. The question's far from a black-and-white one.

Casement What do you call yourself?

Youth James Anderson.

Casement (*speech gradually modulating toward his formalized regionless Irishness again*) Well, Jamie, hear you me. Three hundred and fifty years ago perhaps a da of yours was deported from his own lands and planted where you live now: for a purpose nowt to do with rights of yours. Does Ireland suck at your heart? Yours is a brave inheritance. Dis-sent. Time and time over it has been used, and honed, and used, and never, never, never in interests of your own. You have not been innocent. Plead no helplessness, seek no extenuation, ask no forgiveness; most of all, ask no forgetting. Just ask yourself one question: James Anderson, who is that? Tissue, stranger tissue, in a volatile body with which you seem not to agree? Are you all that alien now? However unjustly come by at the start, where is your home, the home of your heart, if not in those lands now? To the north of here. In Ireland; in this land. On this land. Do you understand that?

Youth I do rightly. But I'm a hated man here. I'd rather be outright English when I'm here than what I am; a man

77

of any colour I'd liefer be, a leper or a dwarf even, to feel less foreign than the thing I am. Boys, but when I'm south here, I'd give anything, anything to be anything other than the hated thing I am. I feel so hated here, so unwhole; to belong here, I would give my heart.

Casement Then give your heart. Your torment of identity is not enviable; but it is the pain of change. You are changing: by that alchemy by which this subtle land defeats in the end all conquerors. You are going down, down into Ireland's blood, her strange mixed drunken blood: be lost in it, the deeper lost, the more you'll find your own belonging. I went this road before, I know how you are torn. But I made some beginning. Follow that.

Youth I am afeared.

Casement Courage you must show. Courage without. Courage within. Delve delve delve deep in your heart, to find it to say: 'I am of this land.' One colour fears another, fears its extremeness. But colours mix. First they must meet.

Ireland, Ireland, transcend this trauma. Sons of Ireland, cease looking for your sunrise in the west. Tear this old bitch Erin off your backs. She'll squeal and claw off skin and flesh from your bones, but rip her off, be free of her: trample her down where she belongs, beneath your feet, to be the land you live from, not your incubus and curse. James Anderson, in that red dawn, come you then down through the Gap of the North. You do not come unendowed. I'll plead with these, to find it in their hearts to say to you: Come in, and look out. Come in.

(Wind soft afar, fading off as:)

Let me lie quiet now. Work for that dawn. Then come with spades, and bring me Home.

DISTRIBUTION OF PARTS

As some guide to casting, I should mention that in the broadcast the parts were 'doubled up' as follows:

Casement/Diarist

III, V Author

V Angry Republican Voice; VII James I, Unholy Trinity, Carson; IX Chancellor; X, XI Blackwell; XI Devoy, Pearse

I Irish Voice; VII Ireland, Irishwoman; XI Irish Announceress, Philoprogenitive Mother

II, IV, VIII Crippen; V Angry Republican Voice; VII Lord, Craig; IX German Vulgar Crier, Meyer; XI Hussey, Tone, Parnell

II Lynch; V Angry Republican Voice; VII Pitt, Lord; IX Third Irish NCO, Monteith; X, XI Sullivan; XI MacCarthy, O Connell, Cardinal

I Neutral Voice; II Mahoney; V Belfast Student, Angry Republican Voice; VI Indian; IX Irish NCO, Clerk; XI Captain, Shanahan, TCD Student, Pikelad

V Angry Republican Voice; IX Second Irish NCO; XI Collins, Youth

V Mrs Begley; XI His Mammy

I, II, III, IV, V, VI, VIII, IX English Announceress ⎫
IX German Announceress ⎪ were
⎪ each
VII World-at-One Commentator ⎬ played
⎪ by
VII World-at-One Commentatress ⎪ themselves
VI Joan Bakewell ⎭

IV, X Irish Air Hostess; V Young Irish Lady; XI Mary Gorman, Holy Sister, Professional Irishwoman

V Anglicized Irish Girl; XI Child, His Ma

VII Bess; X Gertrude; XI Second Holy Sister

VII Tory, Asquith; IX Wedel; XI Asquith

I, VII Crier; II Balladeer; VII Tory; IX Guard, German Voice; XI Ryan

I British Public; III Chalmers; VII Churchill; IX Guard, German Voice; XI Second TCD Student, Screaming Child

I Man in Street; VII Marvell, Lord; IX Adler; XI Cockney Warder, Boy, Clontarf Soldier, Fenian

VII Cromwell, Tory; IX Blücher, Guard; XI Aitken

VII Englishwoman; XI Third Holy Sister

VII James II, Unholy Trinity; IX Fourth Irish NCO, Jagow

I English Voice; III German Voice; VII England, Unholy Trinity; IX German Brigadier; XI Darling.

Fifteen male voices altogether, ten female. A few parts, to be found in addition to these, in the text here published, were cut in the broadcast. They are: IX Findlay, Official; XI Arthur Lynch.

THOUGHTS ON STAGING THE PLAY

There could hardly be a more radically radiophonic text than this one: yet I hope that, in one physical staging or another, the play itself can enjoy a continuing life.

Until I do a proper adaptation, certain guidelines for staging this radio text might be of use.

The simplest, if least inventive, form of stage presentation is by the 'oratorio' method, the actors or readers seated in a semicircle, Casement himself in the centre, probably in consular white. This method of presentation throws all the emphasis – where I think it should be – on the text. But it won't satisfy a director who wants to create a full-blooded show.

Once we venture upon more 'dramatic' modes of staging, several difficulties arise. To grapple with these is something a resourceful and serious director might wish to try. But the difficulties are not all obvious. If many of my thoughts here are prompted by the Royal Shakespeare Company's recent experiment with the play, it is because that production – with all the valuable things it did contain – brought these difficulties clearly to the surface.

The text's verbal nature, for instance, is not in itself a difficulty. What makes it a difficulty is its tissue-like nature, so many subtle resonances rising from and across it. The stage seems a comparatively unsubtle medium for a text like this: much of this subtler vibration gets lost, and the play is thereby diminished. Whether this is inevitable, I do not know. Two factors contribute. The play is polemical; there is much in it of contention and discomfort for an audience in the British Isles. Once actors are physically carrying this polemic, and having to project it out and up at the house, there is a danger that the tone of the evening will become strident and aggressive; the audience will then have good reason to withdraw whatever goodwill they came with. The other factor, related to this, is in the nature of the medium for which I wrote the piece. Because it was to be heard in a box, I set most of the action *in* a box – this was the best way for me to fix those boundaries within which my inner ear could most effectively work. You can see from the page, there is hardly ever a voice raised; you can see how fractional, but telling, are the differences between one broken accent and another in sequence IX; Casement's range of emotional colours might be colossal – but the vocal palette is largely *internal*. A radio actor (a thoroughly professional and very skilful class of man) need only shift his voice by a thousandth of an inch as it were, to achieve a resounding change of effect. The stage-actor needs to use a much larger voice-box: a result of which could well be that much of the quiet wicked anatomising phonetic sardonicism of the play will leap out on the stage in operatic splashes. I think this is a pitfall that must be avoided, if the director and company are truly to serve the play.

Another immense difficulty lies in the play's structure. Even in radio terms I took great risks: a timespan of two and three-quarter hours, played at my insistence without an interval; the long unrelenting crescendo of the history sequence; what is virtually a forty-minute monologue for Casement in sequence X; and so on. There could be no break in the broadcast because I wanted to achieve, in one long span, a sense of the various 'bloodstreams' of the play gradually and indeflectibly achieving confluence. On radio these gambles paid off. In the theatre there are physical reasons why this structure might not hold. For one thing, for audience and company alike, there has to be an interval, and that must come before sequence IX. Again, the monologue of X is possible for a radio actor because he can record it section by section, and establish for himself a fresh threshold at the beginning of each take; a stage Casement has to manage the whole course of it in one clear run, and may find it calling for changes of focus and gear he simply cannot make. In fact, it is towards the end of the play that the structural problems seem most acute. In the theatre this solemn and melancholy mood cannot be sustained for long. Once Casement's coffin at last reaches Ireland, an audience may well think the story is all told – which it certainly is not. They will become, like Casement's judge, 'increasingly impatient' as they have to sit through all those visitations and apologies. Their backs will be in no mood for the extra straw of that crucial final homiletic with the 'patriot not yet born'. In the theatre indeed sequence XI seems to cry out for some last explosion of physical black comedy to clear the melancholy air and give the audience a respite before the serious business of that final duologue. What the RSC and I finally did, instead, was to cut out the 'apologies' and reduce the 'visitations'. Lynch, Sullivan and Asquith said their pieces to Casement after his hanging at the end of X. The Boy and His Ma, the TCD Students, Nuns and Professional Irishwoman followed the coffin from the airfield, with Mac Aulay, FitzGerald, the Screaming Child, Pikelad, Parnell and Pearse weaving around the procession in a gradually evolving Dance of Death. This brought us to the graveside in next to no time, where we played up the comedy of Casement's refusal to be buried there for all we could: thus 'earning' the concentration we needed for the closing scene.

Other structural changes we made at the RSC do not, in retrospect, so much convince me. But they are tempting, and seem logical. I should thus point out what I think the dangers in them are.

The Author's lecture in V was broken up, and parts of it transplanted. It was a virtue of Terry Hands' RSC production that the various dimensions of the play – coffin, lecture, Foreign Office, history etc. – were physically present throughout, so that they could be switched on whenever we wanted. And to have the Author himself thus available throughout the action does seem in essence a good idea. There is however one danger. The 'lecture tone' he adopts in V is acceptable if you hear it once; it becomes less welcome to an audience each time it recurs. Sequence V is better left where it is, to enable the Author, at that critical point in the action, to spell out his personal responsibility for this Casement he portrays, and to present his reasons for thinking about the controversial *Diaries* as he does. Casement and the *Diaries* are, after all, a subject of continuing bitterness. The violence at the end of the sequence, it might be wise to cut.

A second structural experiment that might seem logical and was tried at the RSC, is to have various aspects of Casement shared out between different actors, so that his disparate personae are separately embodied. The Author figured in this, acting as a kind of 'inner prompter', guiding Casement around the landscape of the Congo and his own awakening emotions. There was a third actor involved, who incarnated Casement's superego Foreign Office aspect. It was well brought off, but as an idea it is too schematic to have life, and its final effect was arid. The 'superego' figure underwent an interesting development: he reappeared as Leopold, Findlay, the German Chancellor, Blackwell, Asquith and – nice touch – the Cardinal at the end. But in his Foreign Office persona a problem arises. You cannot forge a true character out of those caricature lines so grotesquely coined by Casement. *Casement* can caricature Percy or Villiers or whomever, because to caricature is to criticize. Villiers cannot criticize himself. Altogether, therefore, this distribution of Casement's personae between several actors, for all its attractiveness, has the effect of diluting the character's complex force; and I do not recommend it.

A third major reconstruction was in the history sequence, VII. Again, it was divided up and interleaved throughout the play. I find two dangers in this procedure. As with the Author's lecturing voice, the tone of the history is less welcome each time it returns. And, by turning the history into a kind of counterpoint, it has the paradoxical effect of making it seem *less* relevant than more. VII is crucial, and crucial where it stands. It serves as a dramatic analogue to Casement's awakening to the Congo- and Putamayo-like predicament of his own land. (The Casement of VIII is much further advanced in rebelliousness than the Casement of VI. This is because the 'illumination' of VII has happened to him in between.) On the stage, therefore, Casement himself must be associated with the history in some way. It must *happen to him*. So the staging of VII presents, as I see it, two main problems. A director will almost certainly want to reduce its text (or thin out its textual density). It will call for considerable insight to do this intelligently. Until he can decide exactly why each item is there, he is in no position to decide which to cut. As to physicalisation, I think the sequence affords numerous possibilities. The RSC used a central rostrum for Ireland, on which invasions, battles etc were formalized. This rostrum began, most effectively, to split in two when Carson came along. Casement himself was on the run the whole time, burdened beneath an accumulation of various cultural insignia – druidic robes, Celtic Christian and Romish vestments, sashes and so on. (This, however, identifies Casement with ancient Ireland – which is historically misleading.) I feel inclined toward the idea of an inexorably circulating procession; the dates, perhaps, on placards; the use of an outline of a map. Perhaps the whole sequence should be presented as a dream Casement has, in which he becomes increasingly embroiled: 'history is a nightmare from which I am struggling to awake.'

The journey of Casement's bones is easily physicalized. The RSC company wheeled him round in an open coffin, with Crippen on the trolley, stopping at each 'station of the crossing' as it were. (He was therefore able, in V, to interrupt the Author's lecture.) Another good RSC idea was to have, in sequence III, not the *Diaries* brought out for the Author to investigate, but Casement himself, wrapped up in papers and hung with labels, from which the company then read out the transposed Who's Who facts of sequence I.

To achieve a good orchestration in performance, I think a minimum company would be about fifteen. The broadcast used over two dozen, and as a guide to casting I give this distribution on page 79. To manage with ten, as the RSC did, is obviously possible, but I think it overstrains the company. Actors need respite, if they are to have the energy fully to inhabit (rather than caricature) these multitudes of flickering characters as they come and go. Casement himself should ideally be an authentic Northern Irishman (for more than mere vocal reasons). He should also avoid camp, except perhaps for a faintest shade of it in the first scene with Wedel in IX. The Youth of the closing pages *must* be authentic; and he is most effective if his voice has not been heard at all till then.

There should be no sound effects other than as directed in the text. In a theatre, indeed, not all of these will be needed. The 'poetic' and 'weird' sounds are, however, part of the texture of the play – the windsounds, the electronics, for instance: these should, I think, be tried for. The audience need an occasional 'cushion', as relief against this very dense text. For a similar reason I think the announcements and scene-settings are essential in live performance; they enable the audience to relax their concentration somewhat. The Mahler march in XI is indispensable, being there not only to move our hearts, but to carry our sentiment over, into the dimension of the dead.